AF255894

Soul of the Painter
David Taylor and Aesthetic Personality

— a monograph —

by Paul Butler

To David
friend, mentor, visionary

CONTENTS

"Fry's use of the word *spiritual* ... what is involved is essentially the operation of transmutative mind in the manifestations of sight, the bestowing upon these of the connotation of a distinct "spirituality," or sense of heightened visual and psychic activity." — David Taylor, "The Aesthetic Theories of Roger Fry Reconsidered"

"...the emotions which tend to characterize the aesthetic selfhood of the mature Cézanne are clearly emotions centred on the expressive potential of his medium ... [these] may very well be as passionate and intense as those experienced in a purely social category, but they would seem to be generically distinct from the emotions of the artist's fellow men, or non-artists." — David Taylor, "Aesthetic Personality"

Applicants for painting classes at the Art Gallery of Toronto, (now the Art Gallery of Ontario, aka the "AGO"), looked to be impossibly numerous. Rather than take a chance, a young, aggressively determined elementary school student named David Taylor, with little more than renditions of Viking warriors in his portfolio, queue-jumps in order to ensure himself a spot. Cross-examined in adulthood as to this behaviour, he retorts, adamantly unrepentant: "I wanted to be a painter and I wasn't going to risk failure."

By the age of fourteen, when most teenagers are mired in a fog of adolescent fantasies, David Taylor had already chosen the long, difficult career path of becoming a university professor in the field of English literature, his second passion. He believed, accurately, that this career choice would provide him with the income to support his art, but more important, the time during the long academic summers and sabbaticals to practice it. Even more astonishingly, this fourteen-year-old recognizes that he wants to produce not domestic paintings, but gallery sized works:

> "By the second year of high school I (perhaps a smart ass) had resolved that I would take a doctorate (teeth sunk in) — needed in this world; a bit odd for the general wildness of fifteen or so. Interested in literature (I had my mother's influence) but — always — the desire to paint — not little things, but someday, something really big — something splendid: little paintings being too restrictive."[1]

His cutthroat tactic appears to have been a one-off. He goes on to establish an overall aesthetic that virtually guarantees keeping him out of the limelight. Other than commissions for portraits and a Tom Thomson copy that he tries to buy back, he refuses to sell any of his paintings.

Taylor's scholarship provides a guide as to what he would have understood by the phrase "a painter's soul": not something of otherworldly import, but rather a descriptive of the direct and immediate experience of the artist at work which is available ultimately to the attentive audience.

> "It is a commonplace to refer to the young artist's apprenticeship to his art as involving the process of finding himself. The nature of the self which he may be said to be trying to find is not too frequently clarified. Much confusion concerning this process is frequently characteristic of young artists themselves. Cézanne … is perhaps, a significant case in point: the instance of Cézanne as a young artist signing very indifferent self-portraits with enormous slashing characters in vermilion — symptomatic

---

[1] David George Taylor, *The Winnowed Field — a brief family history* —(handwritten, bound, David Taylor Archives),194.

of the sort of social élan with which he invested himself as the *enfant terrible* of contemporary Paris — suggests, perhaps more than anything else, the sort of irrelevant, symptomatic self-assertiveness which everybody could, quite happily, do without."[2]

Taylor continues:

> "But after his discouragingly anticlimactic return to Aix, and his emergence from artistic adolescence, such irrelevant emotional gestures tend to disappear in Cézanne's deeper and deeper identification with the real, expressive potentialities of paint."[3]

What appears to have happened here is something like a role reversal: the self-promotion of the immature and socially preoccupied artist has yielded to a disciple's attentive and disciplined sensibility: a disciple's relationship to medium.

Is there not, Taylor argues, a distinction to be made between an artist's sense and discovery of the aesthetic self that is indissolubly connected to and dependent upon the art-making, and the everyday "toothbrushing, neck-washing, breakfast-eating human being?"[4] The artist as artist has no interest in this latter aspect of being. (The reverse can be a different matter. This may very well be the reason why certain members of the breed, when not at their labours, have a tendency to run amok in society, so powerful and liberated do the energies become.)

The argument would go further to say that it is one thing to have an aesthetic eye or sensibility — arguably an attribute that a great deal of sentient life enjoys in varying degrees — and another to fashion aesthetic form and substance, and nurture and develop aesthetic being in consequence.

What then to make of the modern phenomenon of persons who pluck this or that from the spillage of everyday life and proclaim it to be art and themselves artists? Most anything in existence possesses aesthetic attribute — and so a tip of the hat to Duchamp and his urinal — but this recognition is hardly new. The Japanese philosophy known as *wabi sabi* has long directed attention to the aesthetics of natural and everyday objects, the natural processes and the effects that they undergo and that mark them. To recognize and to appreciate does not qualify one as an artist. Neither does the mere presentation of the object to an audience, however wrapped, beribboned, or proclaimed: the infamous instance of the artist's slept-in bed fetish-like on display and valued in the millions of dollars. Is there not some essential confusion going on here? Art is not whatever the self-identified artist proclaims it to be. An impressive Cézanne signature does not suffice.

On the final step towards Taylor's strategic dream of achieving his PhD, he persuaded the world famous literary critic, Dr. Northrop Frye, to become his thesis director. Taylor then gained permission to present a topic that demanded input from three departments (English, Philosophy and Fine Art) — no mean feat in the heavily siloed humanities faculties at the University of Toronto in the 1960s and early 70s. The thesis topic that created this stir was on the British art critic Roger Fry,[5] "allowed because, no doubt, of Fry's considerable influence on Virginia Woolf and the Bloomsbury Group."[6]

---

[2] David G. Taylor, "Aesthetic Personality" (International Journal of Aesthetics and Philosophy of Culture, Lier en Boog, volume 5/issue 2), 7-8.

[3] Ibid, 8.

[4] Ibid, 7.

[5] David G. Taylor, *Roger Fry, Critic in a Landscape, doctoral thesis,* (University of Toronto).

[6] Taylor, *The Winnowed Field,* 151.

One examiner of David Taylor's PhD thesis was Marshall McLuhan, the media theorist, whose fame was cresting worldwide at the time. McLuhan's comments to the doctoral candidate were particularly relevant because they were based on his theory concerning the response of the human eye to light, texture and colour. Taylor's university studies included whatever courses relevant to his painting are available to him:

> "The supplementary course I have taken with the Delacroix expert, Lee Johnson, in Fine Arts — 'the development of colour theory in the nineteenth century' — has been liberating; my technical knowledge of colour is now filled in — and the knowledge is essential. Then, also, the reading of art criticism (from Pliny down) and aesthetics (Baumgarten *et al* that followed) will have a direct — and indirect — practical use in years to come. *The time has not been a total digression* [from the painting]."[7]
> [italics and insert mine]

In his paintings Taylor goes further, much further than mere scornful dismissals of the antics of artists and the credulous endorsements of the art world as to what does not qualify as art. On three canvases he critiques the work and public persona of Francis Bacon, visually and, in addition, textually on the front and the back of each canvas deconstructing the import of the painter's nihilist aesthetic. Bacon himself was not shy to consign much of the world's art production, historical and contemporary, to irrelevance on the basis of its "narrative" content and of its misguided (to him) claims to inherent meaning and value.

Both artists raise fundamental and determinative questions that are in opposition to each other as to the nature of art. Bacon's mortal sin and disqualification would be his frank dismissal of all things redemptive in life and in art. However debatable may be Taylor's absolute censuring of his contemporary's work, the ultimate logic of it leads him to but one conclusion: its nihilism disqualifies it. Providing all the prosecutorial arguments necessary to engage with its defenders, at the same time he deepens the intensity and understanding of his own work.

Painting after painting by Taylor explores and expands upon the nature of aesthetic and creative being. In his writings and his conversation, he makes the case for the whole work of the creative life to be preserved to its fullest unbroken extent:

> "Yeats's question to the chestnut tree: 'great rooted blossomed,/Are you the leaf, the blossom or the bole?' is just possibly the sort of question that should be addressed to a painter like Rembrandt, so various in his forms, yet so immediate in his spirit — and yet it would seem a decided pity to lose sight of the tree."[8]

And,

> "I think, the sentiments of artists ought to give pause to aestheticians [who wish to evaluate work in isolation — 'process is irrelevant to an appreciation of the product' (Hospers)]. It was the generally inarticulate Turner (referring to his own

---

[7] <u>Ibid</u>, 151.
[8] Taylor, "Aesthetic Personality," 10.

paintings, which he was very much concerned should be housed together after his death) who observed, 'What is the good of them, if they are not kept together'?"[9]

Taylor's abiding concern was to keep his paintings together for their fullest expression, meaning and significance:

"The central philosophic error of supposing the individual work of art an autotelic entity would seem to involve the failure to recognize the simple enough truth that … variety may be an essential feature of an underlying identity."[10]

Carlos Fuentes mused:

"In a sense my novels are one book with many chapters."[11]

Most artists and most lovers of their works would agree.

***

The rough division of this monograph reflects the three major periods of Taylor's work as a painter: identified for the purposes of discussion as the visionary symbolic, the visionary figurative and the visionary landscape. He had the usual artist's allergy to being labelled and pigeon-holed and applied none of these terms himself. He was, however, fully conscious of entering upon different periods in his creative life and explored and discarded descriptives for these.

For the better understanding of Taylor's sensibility, not all the contributing material is consecutive. Just as few stories are simply linear, when circumstance required, he would resort to previous modalities of expression, life going back and forth as it does. The term "visionary" as used to qualify each of these periods is not intended to imply a capacity to see into the future but to indicate "heightened" vision as Taylor references it when he writes of Roger Fry's concept of the visual artist's "spirituality" in terms of "transmutative mind in the manifestations of sight."[12]

Were the term "conceptual" not identified with a category of twentieth century art much of which. as art, Taylor disdained, it would have applied very nicely to the middle period of his work where he places his views or concepts of society within visionary contexts. As it is, since in discussions at the time he himself considered and then rejected the idea of being looked at through the lens of any particular movement, it seemed best to present his work in a manner that does not allow for confusion. While his damning critique in triptych form of Francis Bacon has warranted a chapter unto itself, it belongs very much in this visionary figurative period.

— Paul Butler

---

[9] <u>Ibid</u>, 10.
[10] <u>Ibid</u>, 9-10.
[11] Carlos Fuentes, (The Art of Fiction No. 68, *The Paris Review*, May 15, 2012).
[12] David G. Taylor, "The Aesthetic Theories of Roger Fry Reconsidered" (*The Journal of Aesthetics and Art Criticism*, XXXVI/1, Fall 1977), 68.

CHAPTER I

The Visionary Symbolic

As remarked in the introduction, the artist was fond of citing the example of the youthful Cézanne as an instance of confusion between social and aesthetic personality. (Not that Taylor wasn't prey to early self-promotion — he would tell the story of wearing yellow kid gloves to university classes.) Having taken Northrup Frye's two courses, William Blake and the Bible, Taylor drew upon both for his visual language during this early visionary symbolic period in order to give substance to aesthetic self-discovery and its works. Practical lessons and further inspiration came from the interactions with chosen medium: "deeper and deeper identification with the real, expressive potentialities of paint."

A letter of recommendation from Northrop Frye is instrumental to Taylor's obtaining his first teaching assignment, at Huron College, London, Ontario. It comes with living quarters that adequately double as studio, sufficiently large for him to branch out from early canvases that are of modest, "domestic" proportions and occasional intent.m to branch out from early canvases that are of modest."domestic" proportions and occasional intent.

Taylor acknowledges *Peniel* to be his first "significant" work[13] and the first in a series that treats the creative spirit as subject matter and that he identifies as an artist's "aesthetic personality." He "locks horns" with Northrop Frye (a major teaching device of his mentor[14]) over the concept that is central to his doctoral thesis on the art critic Roger Fry, defending himself with the argument that "aesthetic personality" refers to "the artist <u>qua</u> artist — nothing to do with the romantic cult of personality" that is the elevation of the artist within a social context [15]. "Let me go for the day breaketh," he inscribes beneath the painting's title, drawing upon Jacob's night-long struggle with the angel of God in *Genesis* 32:26. Similarly the artist must "wrestle to the ground" whatever in himself intrudes upon the work.

This painting introduces the technique that Taylor refers to as "fracturing" — swift and exact palette knife application of oil paint to sized and sketched canvas. More and more the effect will become one of a conjured release of multi-hued, aesthetic passion materializing in every knife stroke.

---

[13] Taylor, *The Winnowed Field — a brief family history —*, 146.

[14] Remarked by Dr. Joanne Burgess, another of Frye's graduate students at the time.

[15] *The Winnowed Field*, <u>op. cit.</u>, 137.

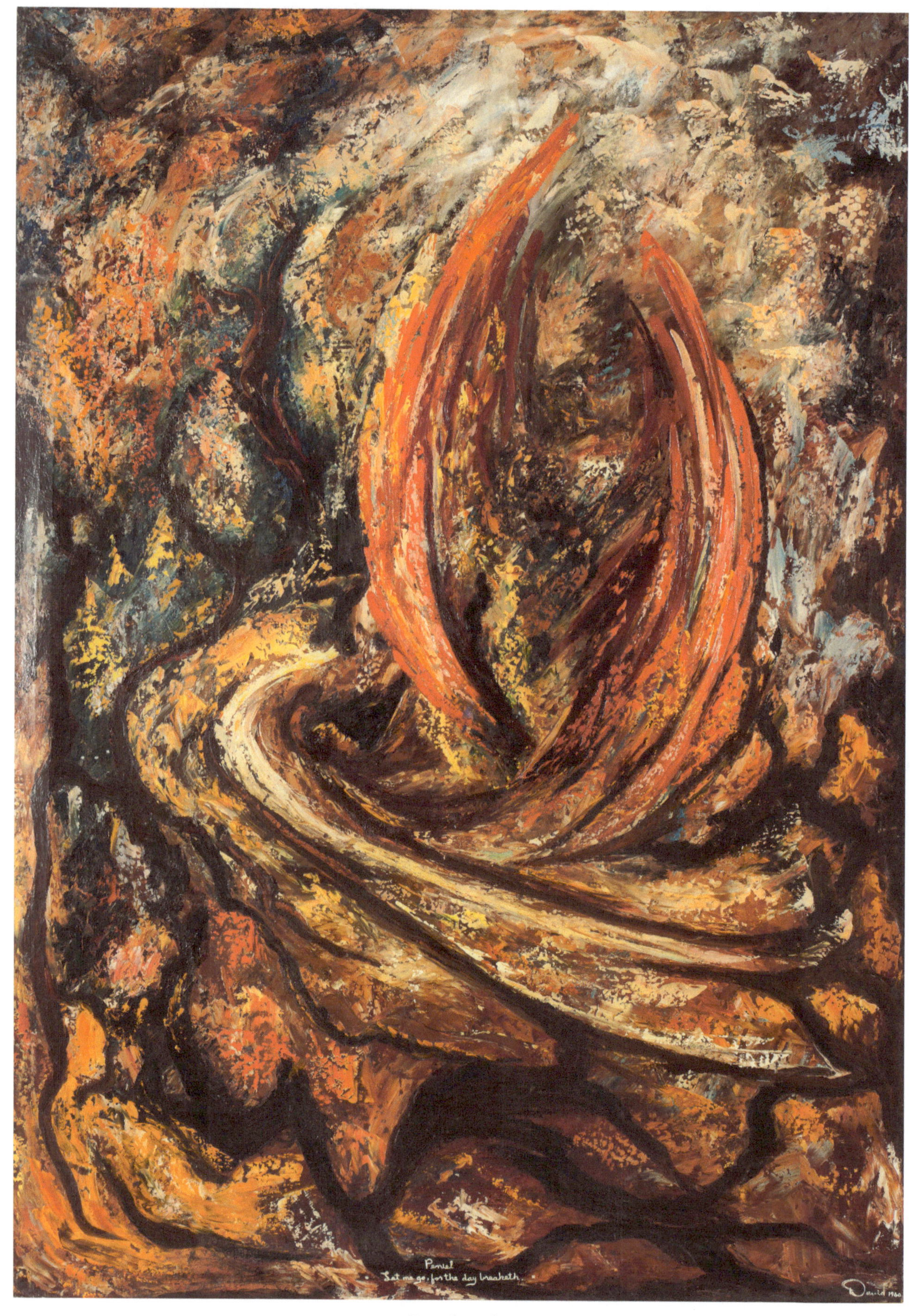

Peniel, 1960

Taylor's first studio directly down from the steeple and to the right

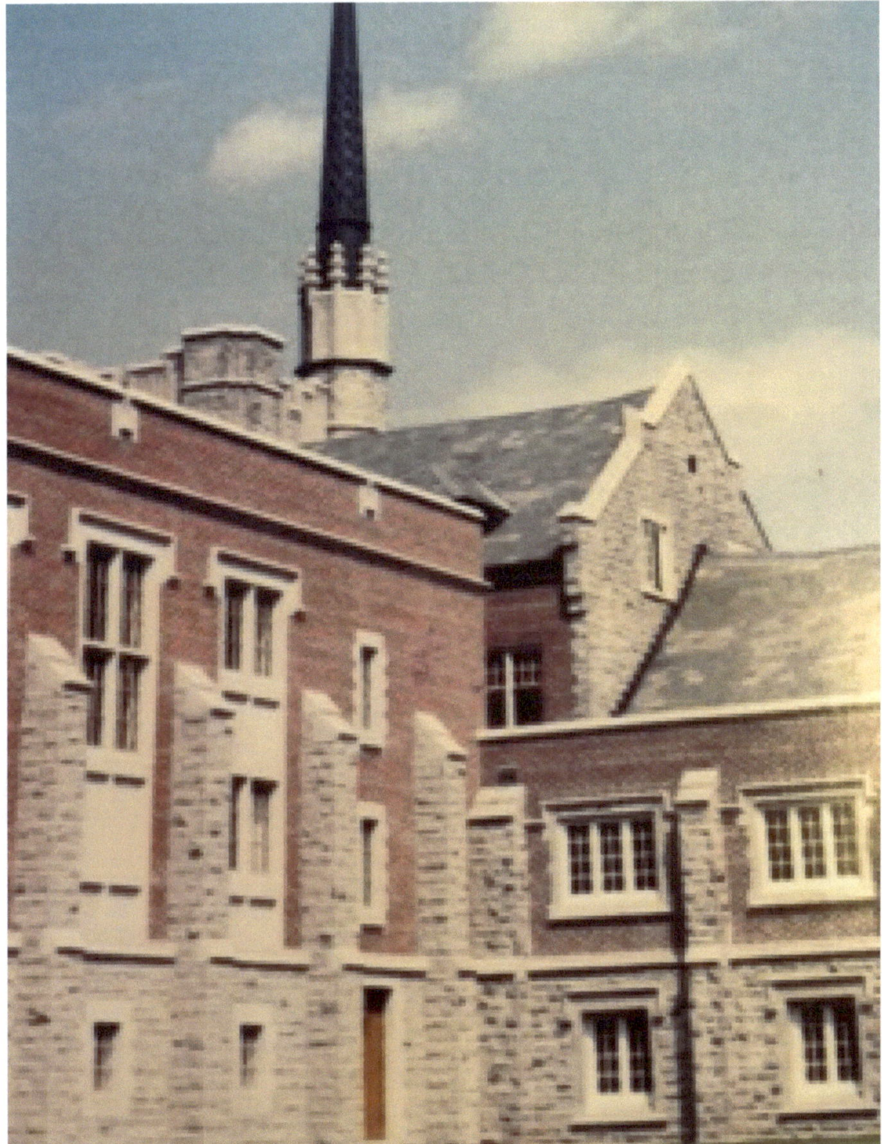

In the mid-sixties, the artist has a first and, as it turns out, only showing during his lifetime "at a Unitarian Church that caters to the arts"[16] on St. Clair Avenue in Toronto where he has to take down his paintings under threat of police intervention. Northrop Frye, at the time Taylor's doctoral thesis director, is invited by Dr. Joanne Harris Burgess, another graduate student of Frye's and also Taylor's officemate at McGill University's Department of English. Northrop Frye comes to the exhibition with alacrity, and is warmly enthusiastic. He later comments, according to his former graduate student, that the circumstance of a Unitarian Church's refusing to host what it found to be "religious" material is ironic in the extreme.

Taylor takes as much affront at religious fundamentalist labelling as the subject of his teacher's Fearful Symmetry would have. He writes in his family memoir:

"Northrop Frye's book on Blake is something I devour — praised as it is by Dame Edith Sitwell as a book 'fiery in its understanding'." (p.136)

The primal creative energies it depicts will be his constant struggle and source of inspiration. They are implacable, demanding everything of him, and he submits, driven individual that he is, throughout his lifetime brooking no influence that might pose a threat, suffering and triumphing accordingly and in private.

In the Biblical passage Jacob receives a wound to his thigh but in Taylor's treatment there is no evidence of it, neither is there of a human figure entirely absorbed, as he must be, by the creative life-and-death struggle. The contest between the immortal divine and the mortal aspirant inevitably leaves its mark but at the same time draws out matching energies.

For the artist, the painting that succeeds *Peniel* is both a revelation and complete declaration of the energies that have emerged in the earlier struggle and that now announce themselves in all their creative, self-sustaining

---

[16] "Located at St. Clair Avenue and Avenue Road," Toronto, Ontario. <u>Ibid</u>, p.180.

power. Inspired by a reading of two editions of *The Revelation of St. John the Divine*, the "large rough outlines [are] … thrown down. Then, as the thing progresses, the original idea is abandoned, something else being dictated. A standing of ten hours — through one night and into the dawn — and it is done."[17]

According to Northrop Frye:

> "… the term 'angel' or 'spirit' in William Blake, when not used in an ironic sense, means the imagination functioning as inspiration, and the fact that inspiration often takes on a purpose of its own which appears to be independent of the will is familiar to every creative artist."[18]

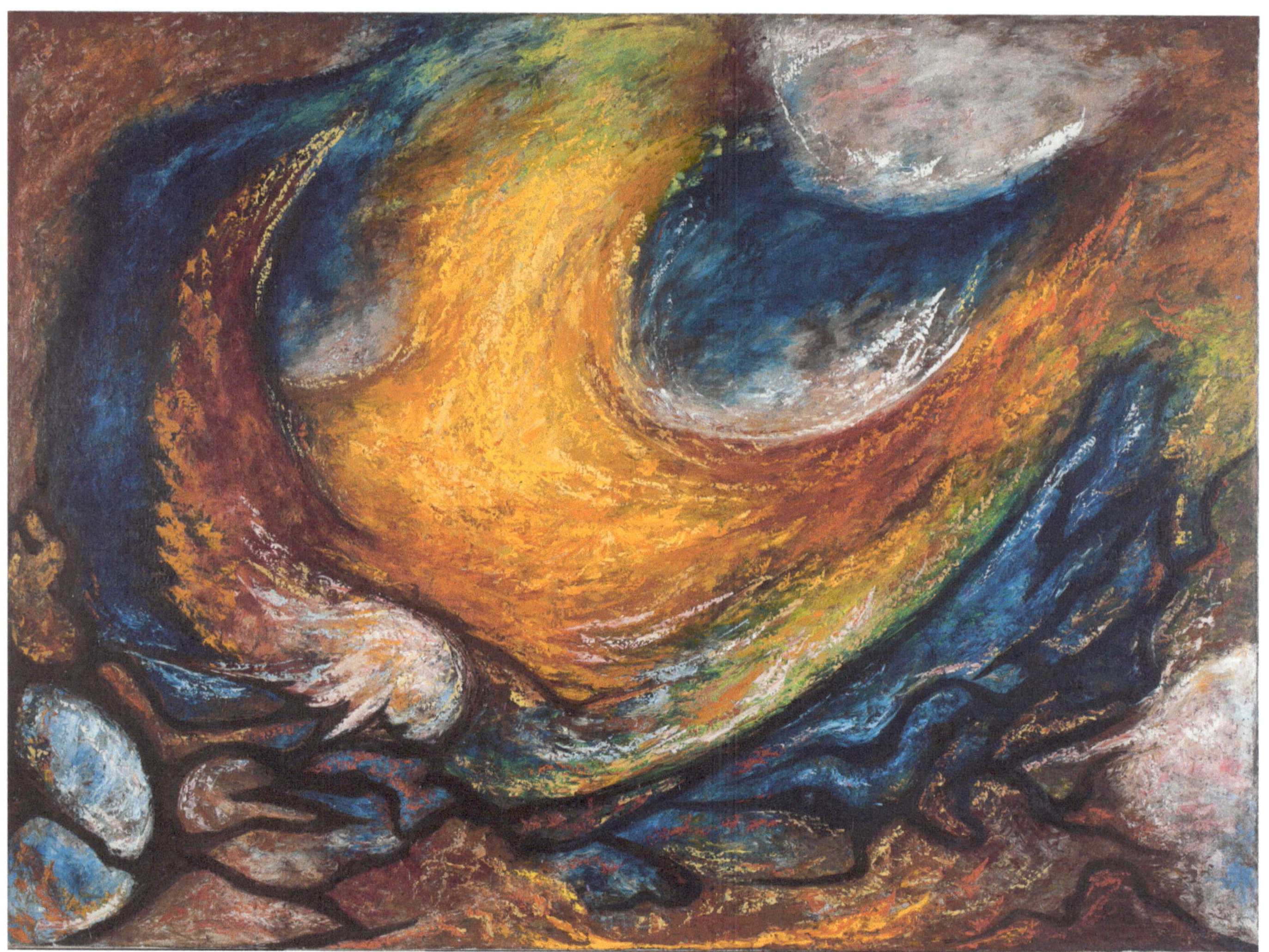

The Sounding of the Seventh Angel, 1960

The result of this "aesthetic process [and its] progressive revelation of merely adumbrative intuitions"[19] is a vortex of whirling colours, textural and resonant that is the artist's early signature work.

---

[17] Ibid, p.146.

[18] Northrop Frye, *Fearful Symmetry: a Study of William Blake*, ed. Nicholas Halmi (University of Toronto Press, Toronto, 2004), 45.

[19] Taylor often speaks of his own painting experience in terms that he applies to Cézanne in his essay "Aesthetic Personality."

14

Taylor expands upon the biblical narrative[20] and has the angelic energy be the agent of transformation as well as its proclaimer; the artist's identity announcing itself and its creative force. Abstracted into an expression of pure transfiguring energy, the sea with its all-inclusive depths and the angel with its revelatory powers appear to be one and the same — an immanent visitation of undying creativity — and something for the viewer to discover as inherent. The concentrated treatment expands visually; its scale is incalculable.

Later, the artist writes:

> "My career as a painter has begun. The Sounding of the Seventh Angel is liked by everyone who sees it. (But where did it come from? — this very powerful image.) Six years later, and in another city, I still cannot find out how I did it. It becomes the standard against which everything is now measured – and, to my eye, fails. A parting of the Red Sea – solid ground revealed; but once passed over – does one really ever pass that way again?"[21]

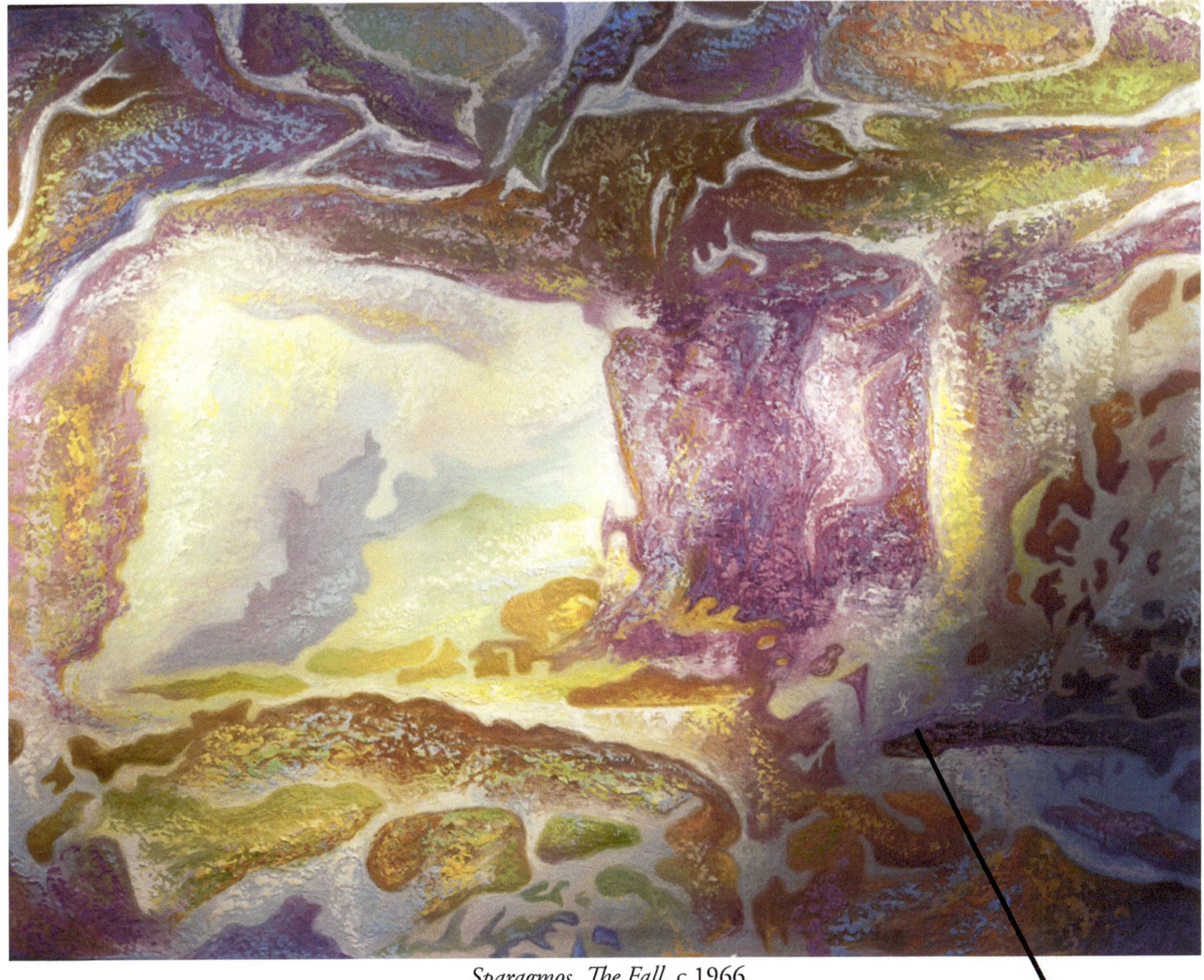

Sparagmos, The Fall, c.1966

fleeing figure

---

[20] *Revelation 11:15*
[21] Taylor, *The Winnowed Field,* 146.

Of the period between this and a complementary canvas, disappointments and betrayals mark his personal life and bring feelings of social isolation. Biography is operating in Sparagmos, The Fall. A tiny figure of the sort that occupies, proportions, and humanizes large Chinese landscapes, flees a cosmic apocalypse. This is not the artist transcending, but his fragile, disconnected, everyday mortal self shattering.

Upon obtaining a lectureship at McGill University, "with the beginnings of a mental illness, generally concealed," he advertises for living/studio accommodation in Montreal.[22]

The response comes from the Marquis de Rusée d'Effiat, an art lover who is renting the top floor of his personal residence located on Redpath Crescent and the upper south slope of Mont Royal.

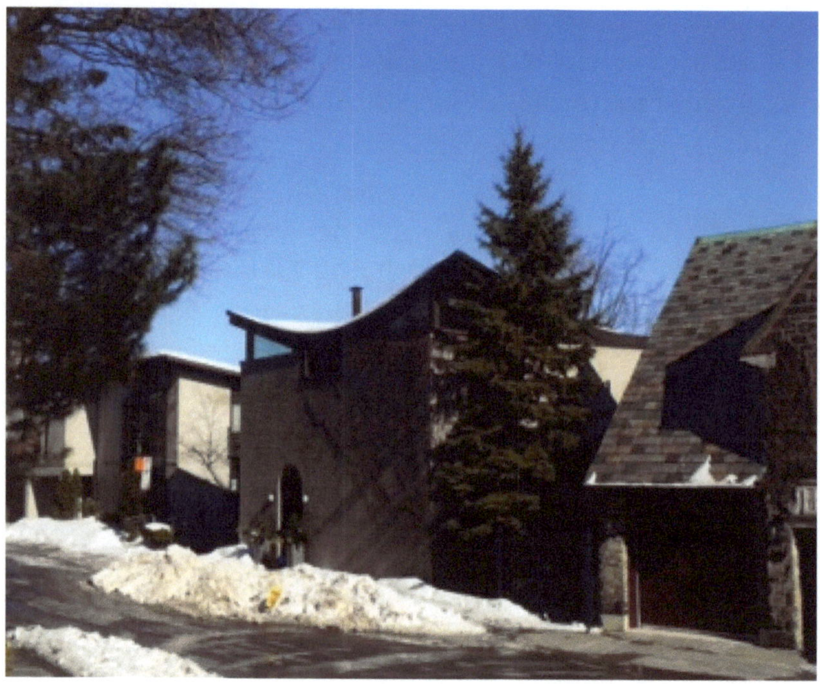

Montreal (Redpath Crescent) studio

***

The Author Encounters Prof. David Taylor for the First Time

Taylor pays no particular attention to the student in the side front row of his first year survey course, not even a glance at the impudence of the outstretched legs, the student's usual over-confident manner. At the end of a class, discussing an assignment, the student lets drop that he writes poetry whereupon, in kindly fashion, his professor offers to look at it. Some days after receiving the submission, Taylor reports back that he has much to say of his findings and invites him to his home that they might adequately deal with these.

With directions in hand, the student climbs the road that coils about the southern slope of the city's Mount Royal. Among the old baronial, cut stone houses he comes upon a flat surface of pale cream-coloured brick with a roof that arches at its corners like uplifted wings; beneath the tips of these, windows receive the outdoor light. The whole of it resembles a couched bird half-raised for flight. On the crescent's south side, it fronts upon the mountain and only two stories appear to the street, but in its rear construction two more levels are cantilevered down the mountain's rock face.

Taylor occupies the top floor where the ceiling slopes upward in line with the roof and the living quarters form a U about the stairwell leading down to the front door. The high rear wall, panelled entirely in glass, commands a wide expanse of the city, the southern stretch of its encircling river, and, far beyond, obscure flatlands and dimly viewed mountains with more than enough sky to liberate thought.

Upon arrival, instead of being engaged in the purpose of the visit, the student finds himself otherwise absorbed. His professor, as it turns out, is an artist and eager to have an audience for his work. Large,

---

[22] <u>Ibid</u>, 151.

framed paintings hang on the walls. At the far end of the apartment, which also serves as a studio, stand even larger, unframed canvases. These monumental abstract renderings are immediate in their effect. One, with its central fiery wave, and executed in a single night, presents the very forging fires of the creative spirit. Another work shows a universe torn apart and collapsing about a tiny fleeing Adamic figure. Taylor comments on Oriental landscape style, with its inclusion of a minute human element that serves to instil an aspect of consciousness and responsibility into Nature's vast presence. Whatever makes the painting's subject matter personal, he keeps to himself. Before these two paintings of the human spirit subject to creative and destructive powers, metaphysics becomes more than mere speculation.

***

The *Seventh Angel* canvas leads Taylor to conceive a triptych in order to expand upon his vision of the artist's relationship to medium. In the central canvas, creative energy towers in a visionary world.

Flaming, fiery, expository, the canvas proclaims the authority of the creative being. Flanked by *The Sounding of the Seventh Angel* on the left side, and the soon-to-be-painted *The New Jerusalem — Building of the City* on the right, it arbitrates between and connects the two paintings. One of the angel's feet stands on land (site of the visionary city), while the other is on the sea (and its creative depths). The painting

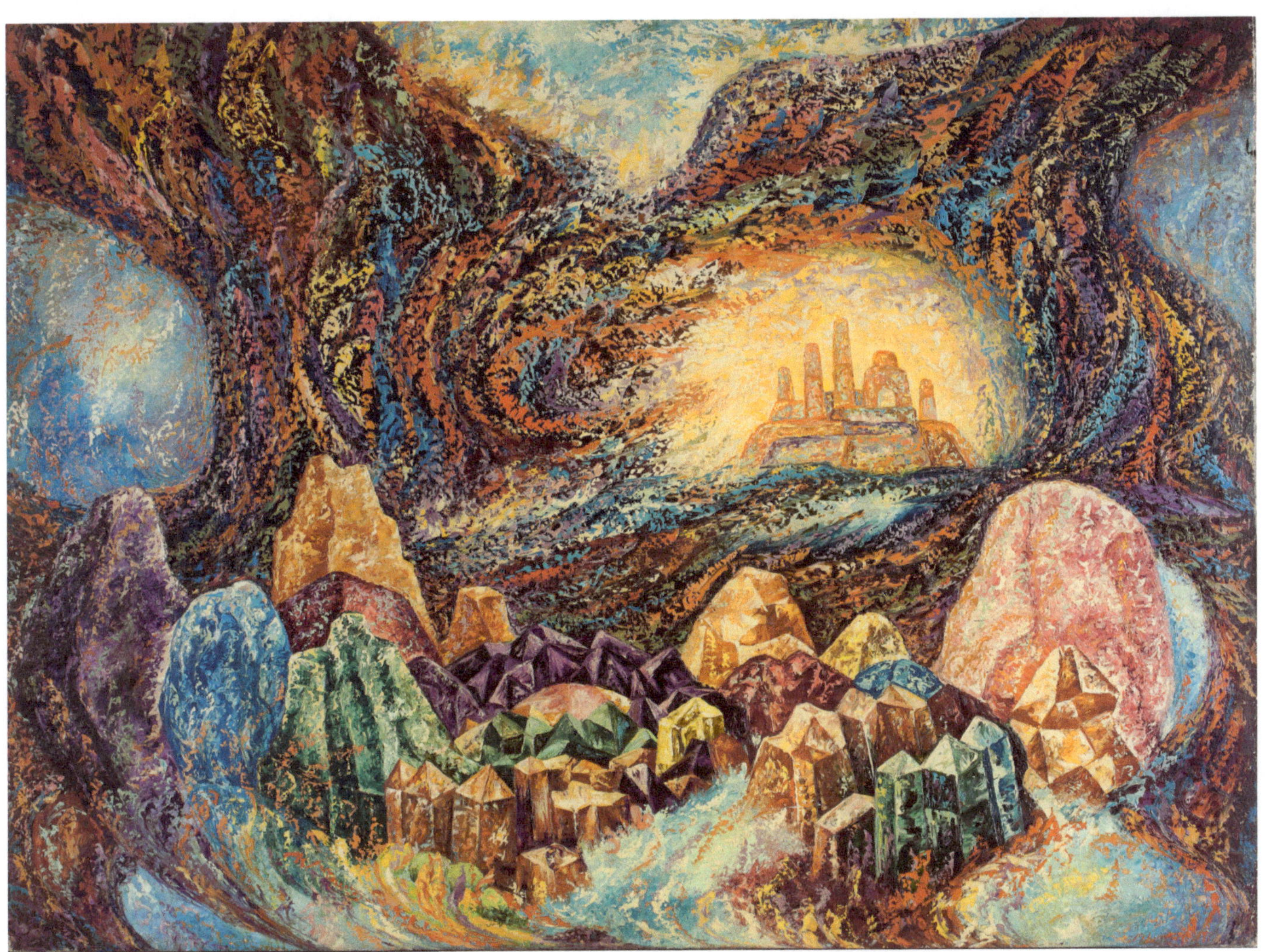

The New Jerusalem — Building of the City, 1967

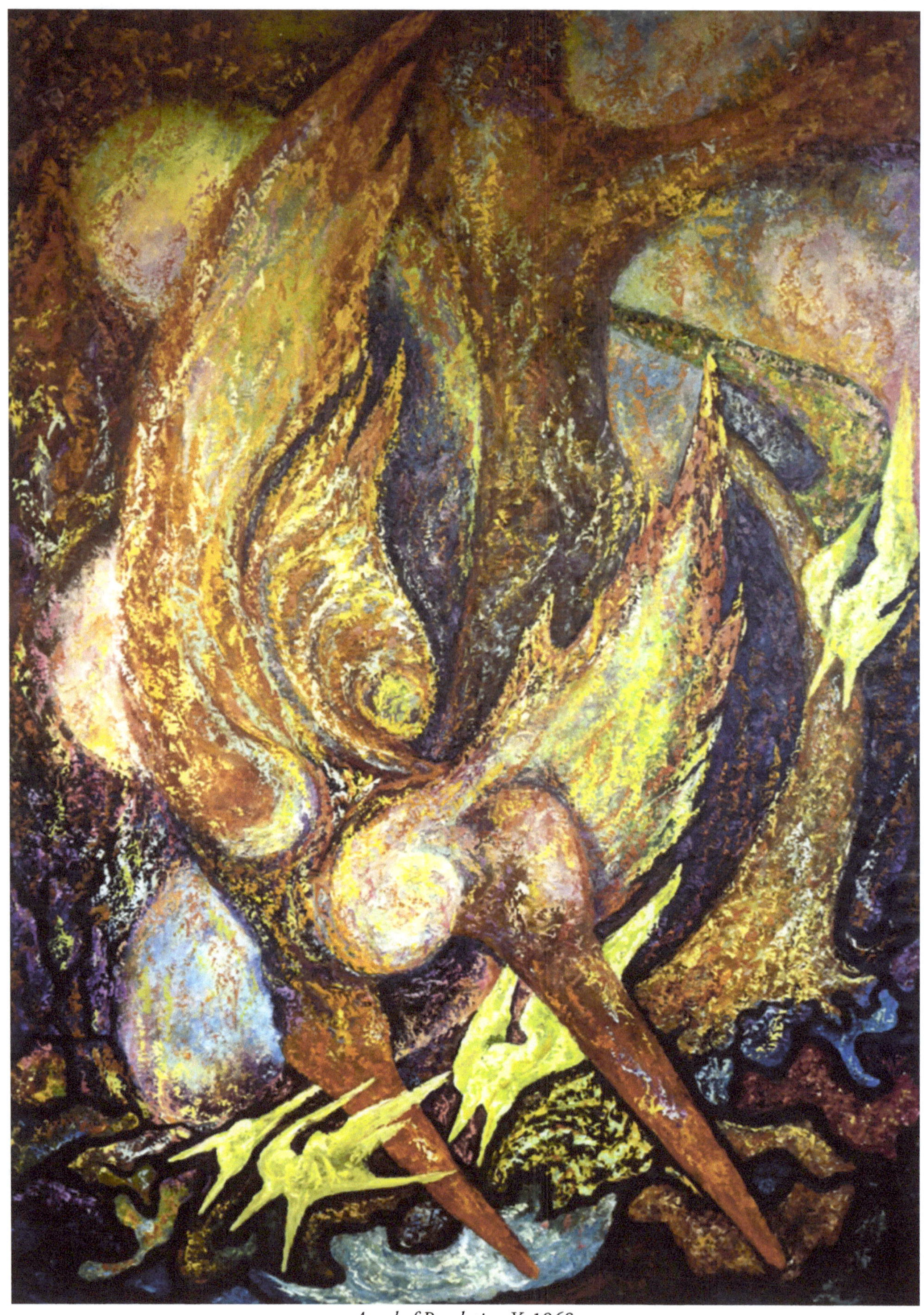

Angel of Revelation X, 1968

draws its inspiration, as do the two companion pieces, from *The Revelation of St. John the Divine*.[23] Embodying creative impulse and thought, fiery equine forms fly between bestridden land and sea.

A vortex of light-centred creative energy holding and sustaining the whole of the realized vision[24] — the "City" — swirls within the right flanking canvas of the triptych, its crystallized foreground either emerging from a lyrically sustaining sea or forming an impenetrable barrier between it and the transcended realm. In both cases, the harmony is complete.

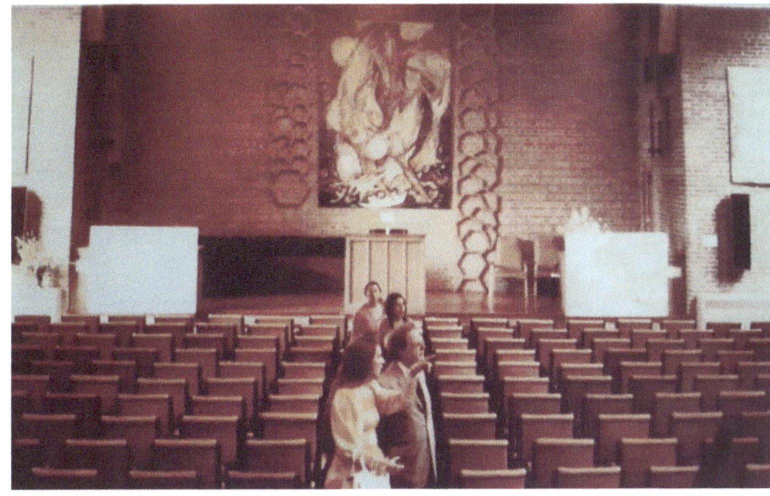

Sole surviving polaroid photo of Unitarian Church exhibit attended by Northrop Frye and Dr Joanne Harris Burgess (foreground). *Angel of Revelation X* is visible; sunlight unfortunately washes out other paintings.

"The highest possible state . . . is not the union of lover and beloved, but of creator and creature, of energy and form. This latter is the state for which Blake reserves the name Eden."[25]

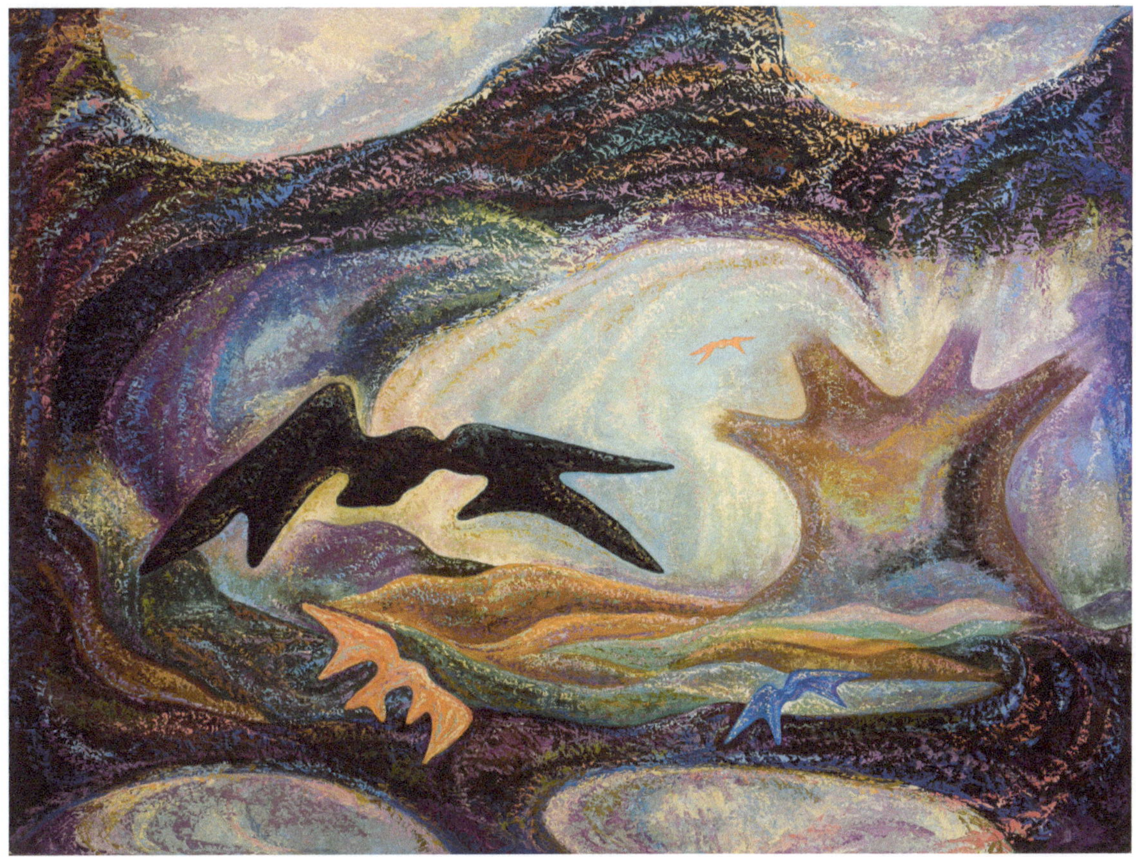

Passage Over Eden, 1969   On the back of the canvas: Part I of Edenic diptych

---

[23] *Revelation 10.*
[24] *Revelations 3:12* and *21:2*
[25] Northrop Frye, *Fearful Symmetry, A Study of William Blake* (Princeton University Press, 1947), 49.

In a symbolic return to untrammelled vision, energy and form are in flux as the artist's thoughts and perspectives strive toward the tree of life that is rooted in the creative ground of its outpouring vision.

It is at this time that Taylor is finishing off his doctoral thesis on the British art critic, Roger Fry. In his research, he comes upon William Turner's lament: "What is the point if they [the paintings] are not together?" This sentiment encourages his own thoughts as he witnesses the emerging interconnectedness of his canvases, for he is to repeat these words throughout his career, so much that they come to express a wish and a directive.

***

Teacher and the student he will mentor have become friends.[26] Accompanied by two female companions, they enter the New Hampshire hiking trails at Crawford Notch and find the first shelter occupied and, despite its being early evening, decide to try for the next one, some five miles down the wilderness trail. They make good progress while the light lasts but it isn't long before twilight is sending its streams of dazzling and silvered colours through the trees. They are plunging on as dusk and then complete darkness fall. When they have to cross a broad stream, the night sky does give enough light that they can leap safely from rock to rock, boulder to boulder. Within the woods, they frequently have to resort to a dim flashlight. At last they come upon a small clearing and the sought after shelter.

They are very taken with the place; the wild tumble of the mountain stream's flow, the boulders and trees, the trails that track the valley as it dips and rises along the mountainside. One evening, seated before a large cheerful fire, Taylor gets out some sketching paper, having seen something worth capturing in the ember-studded arrangement of the burning logs.

(Toward the end of his life, he looks upon the particular painting that emerged with a witheringly dismissive eye, for reasons that would escape any but the apparently select — someone's deprecating critique, so he claims, of some aspect or other, has at last eaten away at his long approval of the work).

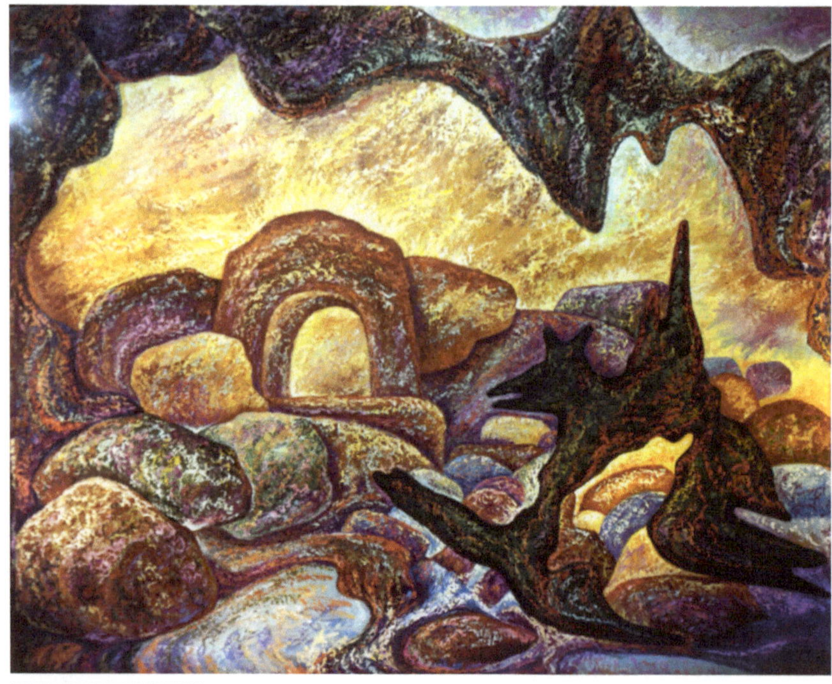

< I, *Ezekiel*, by the River Chebar,[27] 1972

This is no rough, Yeatsian beast slouching to be born. The force of revelation burns in the creature's wonderment at its inflamed world. Both are transfigured. Here is but one of the infinite shapes the soul of the artist may acquire. A similar Arc de Triomphe passage through rock, signifying that this is the way of like-minded beings, here presents as is found in the city of *The New*

---

[26] See Paul Xylinides, *Sparagmos: the fall — a memoir —* (2015).
[27] *Ezekiel 3:15*

Jerusalem, one of its scant identifying features. With reference made to Roger Fry: "the moment anything in painting ultimately depends 'on reference to something outside the picture … it becomes part of an actual, and not a spiritual, reality'." No initial modest campfire. No mosquito-free summer's evening. No Appalachian hiking trail. An artist sketches something he sees above the red coals that is fated to disappear, not unlike the flames themselves, while his oblivious companions sit about.

He comes to regard a succeeding and related painting more favourably, although in later life it is his friend's admonition that prevents his excising it as well from the collection. Knifing away a strip of canvas on the left side diminishes the effect of what he regards as an intrusive element.

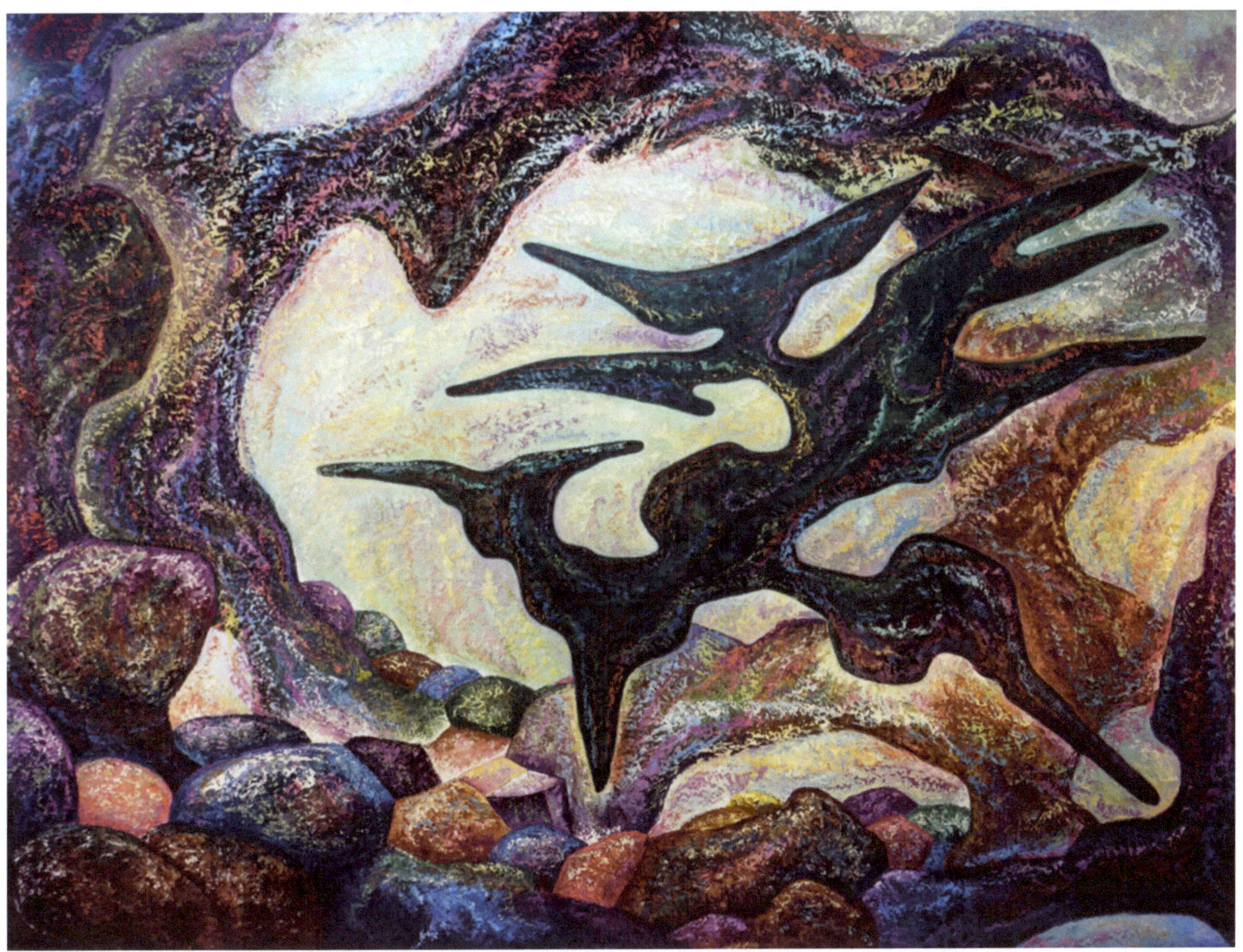

Likeness of the Ox, c. 1973

Also from *The Book of Ezekiel,*[28] the aesthetic being is necessarily one with, yet new to, the vision. Here, the composition, as in so many of Taylor's works, is circular, reminiscent of the biblical prophet's "wheels of fire."

***

---

[28] *Ezekiel 1:10*

A cigar-smoking, expansive and expensively suited uncle in the Alberta cattle business struts about the Montreal studio on an unexplained visit to Eastern Canada and accepts the previously uncontemplated role of patron for a series of canvases beyond Taylor's means to finance at the time. He has no real sense of the work on display but the paintings are big and full of colour and nothing to argue against here: a studio with location, a bright spark of a nephew with a university teaching position, and an internationally acclaimed World's Fair recently in town: lots of reasons to show himself munificent. Sometime afterwards, Trudeaumania of all ephemeral political outbreaks, sweeps the country and Pierre Elliott becomes Prime Minister.

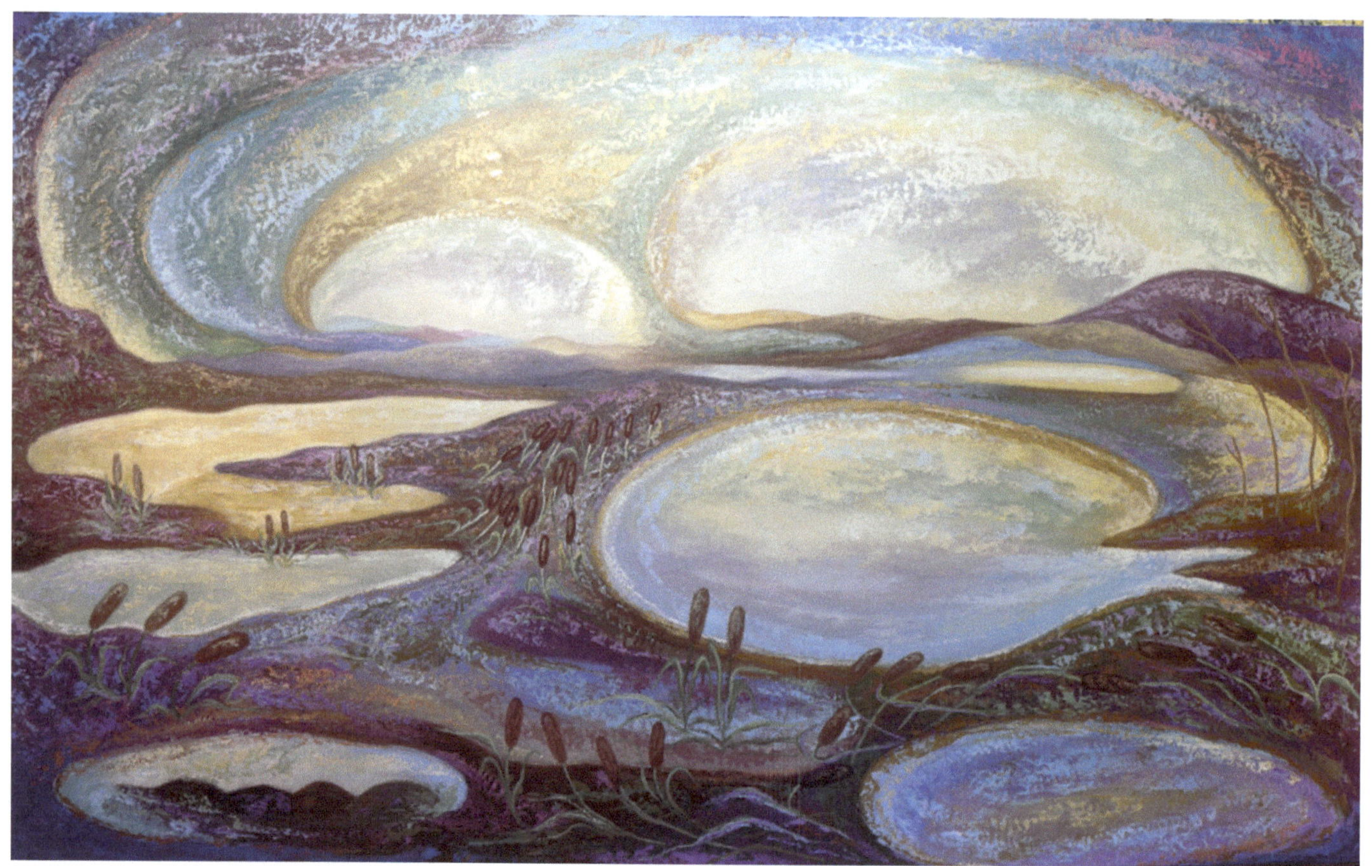

Silence, 1972

Taylor portrays the natural world as rooted in the capacities of vision. The humblest of wind-blown plants –- reminiscent of the baby Moses' sheltering bulrushes — are as conscious of the promise that surrounds them as is the viewer. The painting evokes silence as a sensible presence mediating immanent revelation. It is a subject that he dramatically returns to in a following lyrical work. Eventually, the time will come when he turns full attention to what he sees as intrinsic to the natural world.

Luminous paintings emerge from the avuncular largesse, pure declarations of universal, transcendent consciousness. "How do you know but ev'ry Bird that cuts the airy way, is an immense world of delight, clos'd by your senses five?", *The Marriage of Heaven and Hell* declares.

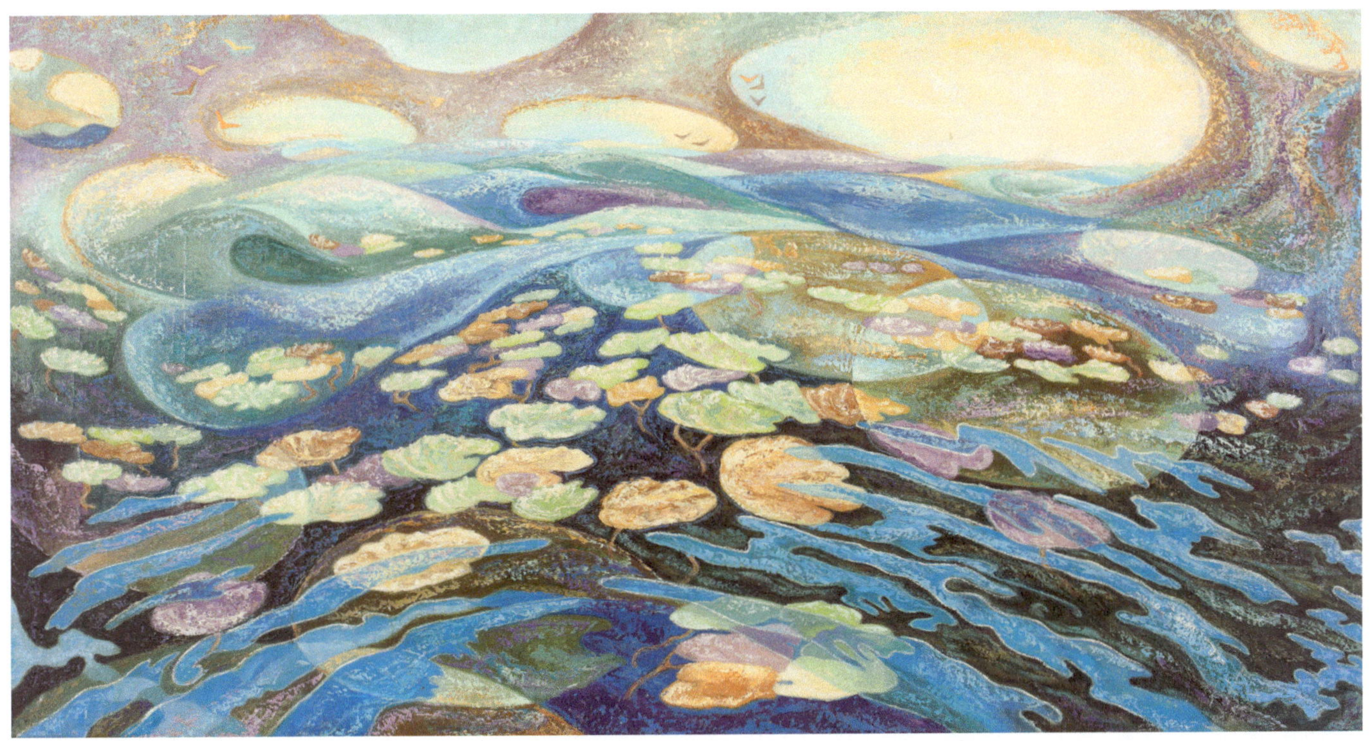

Sea Lilies, 1974

The artist will make assertions as to how aesthetic transcendence comes into being, how it is lost or unrealized, essential questions where heightened vision is under constant threat in the everyday world. Taylor becomes a vegetarian as a young teenager, at a time when it is not a common practice. His sister's dismay at the gasping-for-air fish that he has caught in his net causes him to reassess his behaviour. Conflicted by his uncle's cattle money, he decides it might as well be spent on a good cause and what better than paintings that would otherwise be frustrated by a mere lack of funds? Are not the endless suffering and endless beauty of the world, so closely knitted, an example of this hard truth?

He never makes reference to the lilies' symbology in the painting, whether or not he has drawn upon the tears shed at the Crucifixion, or upon the exile from Eden, or something else entirely. The effect of the Unitarian Church's earlier branding of him as a proselytizer either closes his mouth or he has differently sourced the work's metaphysics. Regardless, it may be enjoyed for its purely lyrical assertion. If one can read of a world where the lamb lies down with the lion, why not consider one where lilies adorn the undulating salty sea? The lift of the waves' sublimely contained energy, the flowers afloat above their probing stems, are the details of a landscape as far removed from mere fantasy as they are from beachfront realism.

***

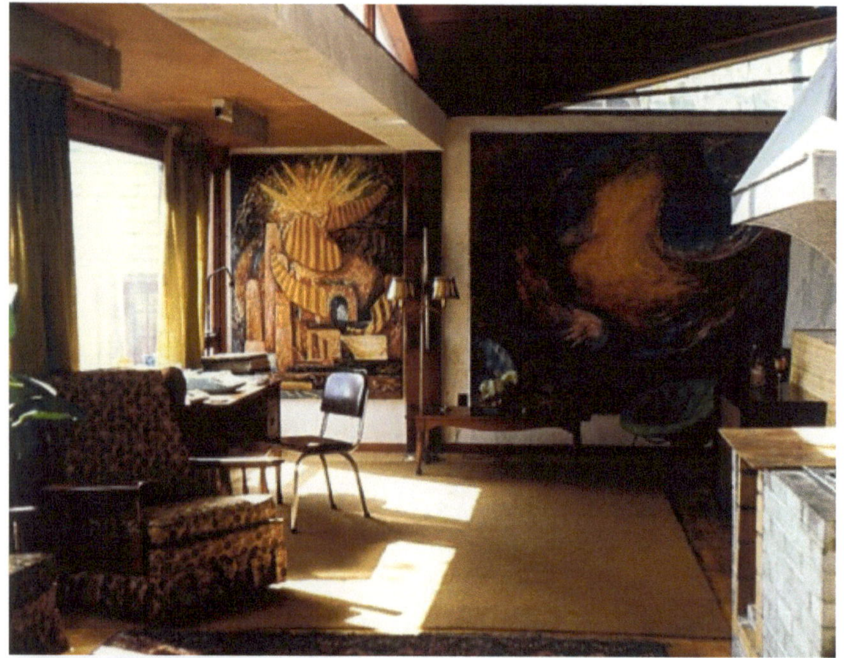

< Montreal studio interior: on the walls, from left to right, destroyed pentaptych painting, and *The Sounding of the Seventh Angel.*[29]

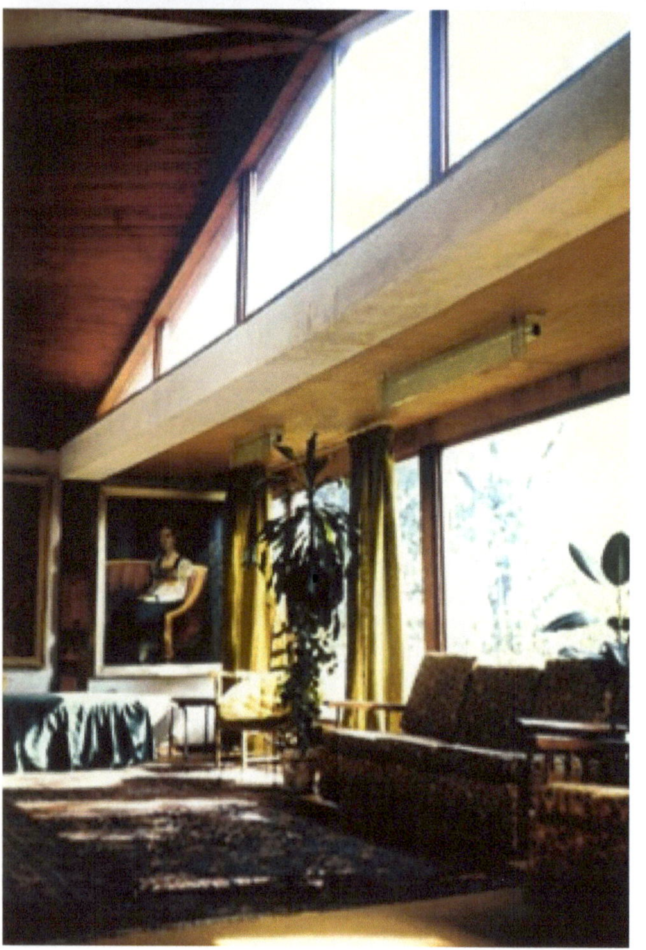

< Montreal studio interior on far wall *Zenobia* (damaged beyond repair)

***

His mother dies and, when his friend returns from a lengthy stay abroad, it appears that Taylor has also lost his studio. A colleague at the university, along with her husband[30] and two friends – one of them a Talmudic scholar – managed to save his work, hauling away the paintings, carefully wrapped, in a large moving truck. His colleague also made sure to cover his art supply debts and take over his classes while he recovered from psychological difficulties sufficiently extreme as to have required hospitalization.[31] She is recompensed with the gift of his painting Silence.

The best explanation for the oversized ramshackle house in the Baie d'Urfé suburb of Montreal, its lack of furniture, making for bleak conditions to view the wind-tossed river, (to all appearances his sole diversion), is the need to accommodate the

---

[29] Taylor eventually drew back from his expansion of the triptych comprising *The Sounding of the Seventh Angel, The Tenth Angel*, and *The New Jerusalem — Building of the City*, into a pentaptych.

[30] Dr. Joanne Burgess and her husband Ian are the friends in deed.

[31] Their most severe manifestation he identifies as "claustrophobic image retentiveness." Taylor, *The Winnowed Field — a brief family history —*, 178.

finished canvases. Ever secretive in his social interactions he doesn't make mention of his claustrophobia as another contributing factor. In the midst of it all he is one of the non-tenured staff that the English department at McGill lets go. He eventually is taken on at Concordia University, and manages to regain his old studio.

His friend returns from a two-year stay abroad and Taylor sets about a plan for the two of them to build a new studio at his Toronto home. He constructs the model of the design in all of its intricacy and attention to detail: floor-to-ceiling bay windows will make up the twelve foot walls on three sides, while cascading skylights descend from two roof planes, side and back. A third large skylight will sit on another side plane. The whole will rest on the lower half of the split-level house in place of the present roof. In the end, the construction eats up three summers: the first to put up the shell against oncoming winter, the second to finish the outside, and the third to complete the interior.

The window-clad, crystalline painter's studio shines at the bottom of the suburban cul-de-sac. People stare and stop to admire, cars specifically drive down on a summer's evening for the purpose of investigation. (In years to come, the giant bays will have to be rebuilt in their entirety owing to the rot that will set in.) The studio's elegance and openness perfectly suit Taylor's need for a self-enclosed world that opens to the one beyond while offering protection from what so troubles him about it.

Interior shot of Willowdale studio >

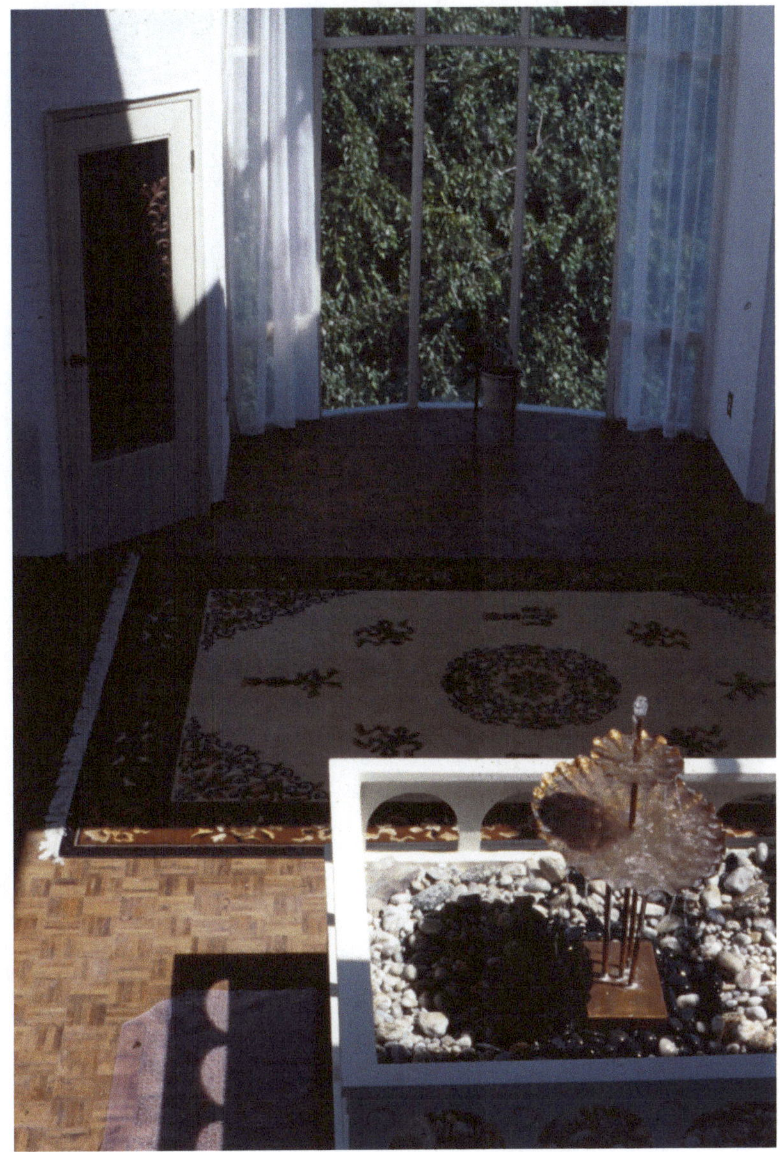

In the centre of the studio, a fountain anchors the huge space and patters onto shells of beaten copper, its never-to-be-met challenge: to cool a seventy-pane fenestrated hothouse. On point duty, a single quixotic fan faces out a high window ejecting a thin stream of heat from the upper regions. Translucent voile curtains, machine-sewn by Taylor, filter the sun's thin yellow blaze, motionless when not catching a breeze through the floor- and window seat-level casement windows, hand-made like everything else, excluding the furnishings: sofa, carpet and a couple of bucket-type seats for guests. Inside his completed new studio, Taylor constructs a scaffold on wheels, inspired by some Roman military design, that he erects and mounts when at work on extra-large canvases.

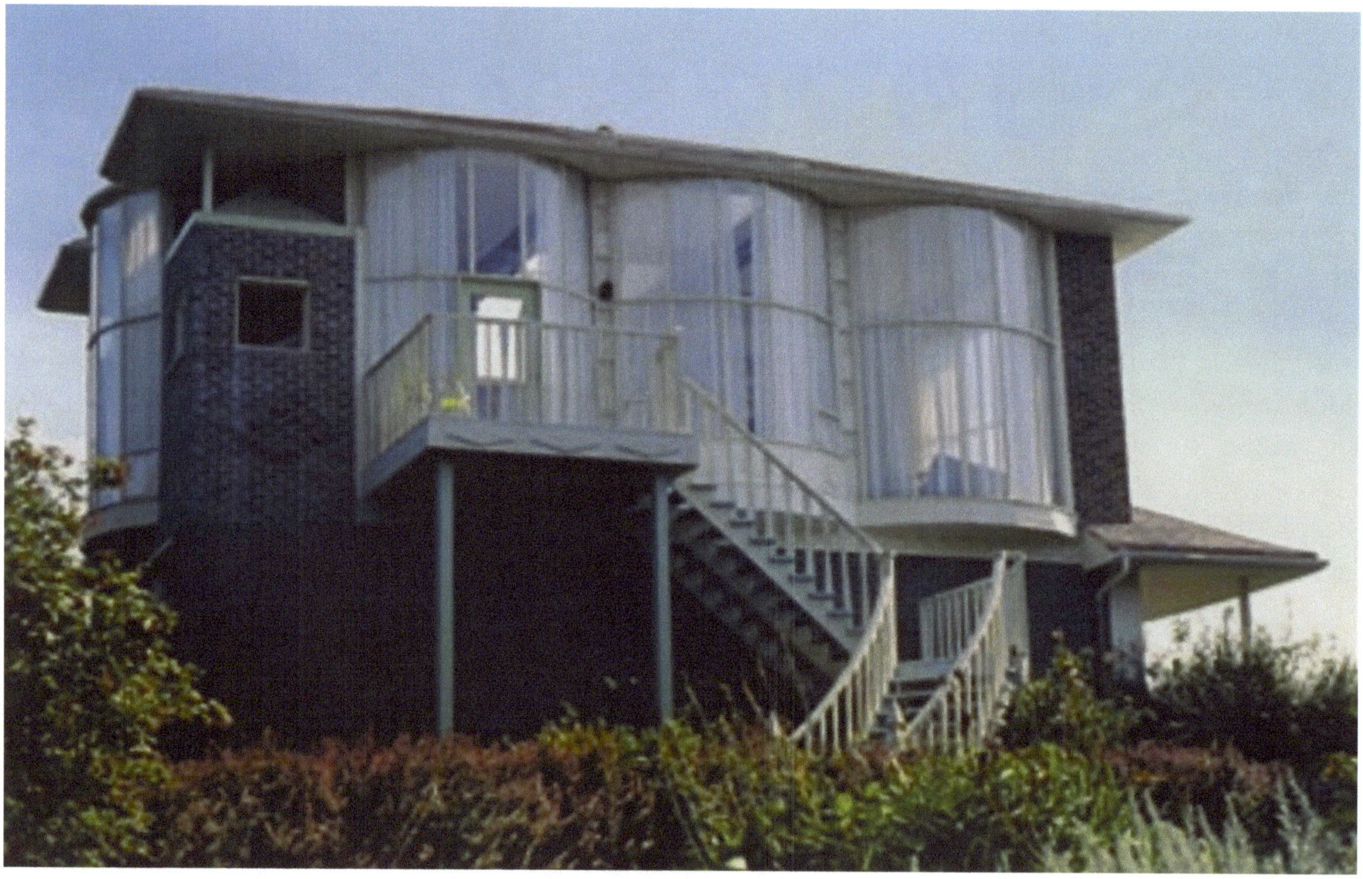

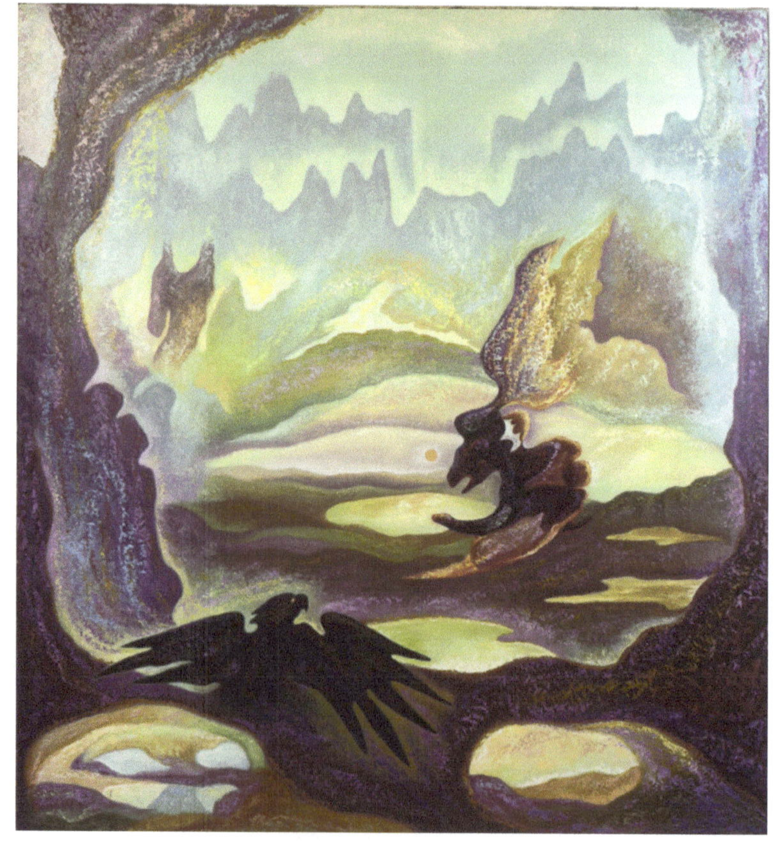

Willowdale studio

Visitation, 1973

No matter the heat or, in winter, the cold, the artist sits on his paint-smeared, wheeled office chair before the latest large-scale canvas, bringing to mind the diminutive human figure in an oriental landscape. When it rains, he thinks to rush about and place an assortment of containers beneath the skylights' various troublesome leaks, whose existence and damaging potential go out of mind once the skies clear. There are always better things to think about and that accord with the preferred state of mind — a personal harmony known only to himself, preserved and defended against all incursions. Months pass without a visitor. Splendid isolation, it's called.

***

As loquacious as one would want on a social occasion, Taylor is content to sit before a canvas such as Visitation for long periods and keep his opinions to himself, more interested in what the viewer sees and has to say.

Where the *Seventh Angel* painting conveys creative energy as a transcendent endowment, *Passage Over Eden* has creative thought and inquiry in avian flight, and the *Book of Ezekiel*-sourced canvases show the artist's being in primal form, in *Visitation* Taylor arrives at its most fully realized embodiment. The aesthetic and visionary energies are self-sustaining, procreative and liberating; a plumed display of thought, intention, emotion, sensibility. No matter that the sun is distant, for the light expands and permeates the most nonmaterial of realms. The creature is self-formed. It has shed its "physical" body — perhaps the truncated brown shape that hovers like an air-hung gown long-discarded (left side) or a long-dead tree of earthly knowledge (a familiar symbol in Taylor's work[32]). The energies are those of the artist in revelatory concert with his medium that calls upon the viewer's matching nonverbal responses. This beckoning visitation seeks in all confidence its kind.

Referencing the interchange, in abstracted departure, between Michelangelo's anthropomorphized God figure and the Renaissance artist's made-from-mud Adam (Sistine Chapel), creative energy reaches out of the starlit darkness in *There Is No Constancy in Time: Reject It*, reaching (upper right) down to touch an emergent, inchoate being, insouciant and sure-footed, balletically inclined.

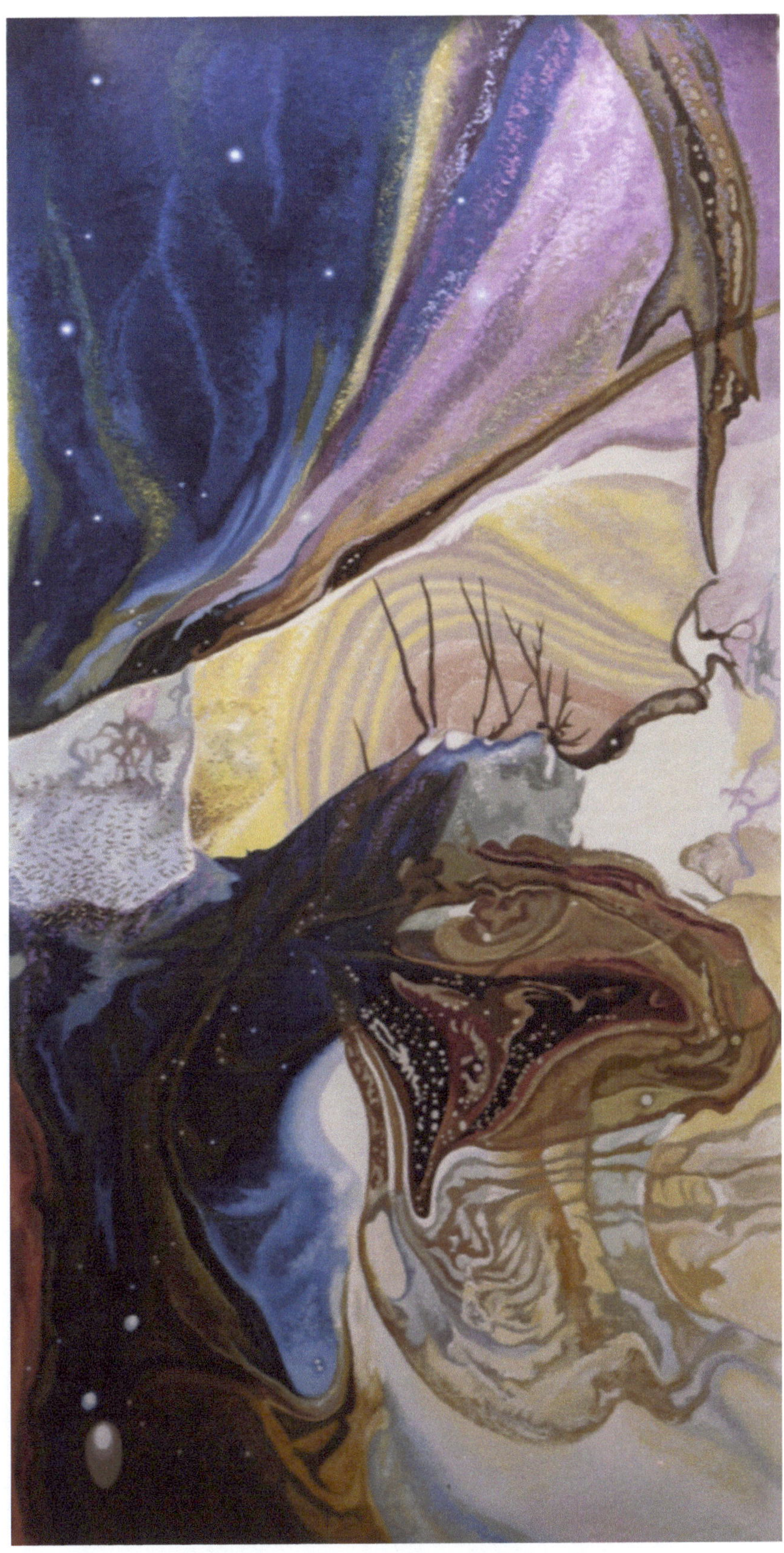

There Is No Constancy in Time: Reject It, 1981
(The artist destroys an equally monumental companion work.)

---

[32] Compare the contrasting treatment of the same image in Passage Over Eden (ch.i, The Visionary Symbolic) and The Universe of Francis Bacon II (ch.iii, David Taylor vs Francis Bacon, The Visionary Figurative cont'd).

The perceived cosmos, not earth-centric, is on its stubborn, turtle-like, implacable way; the new emergent life form under cosmically generative attention occupying a golden vein of primal dawn that slashes across recognizable ground in the canvas's rising middle ground. Trees without branch and leaf reach upward as though oblivious of the bird-filled blue sky and its riving, brown-swirled, pink-capped warnings of quantum shift. Does Taylor, who can rarely shake off a censorious memory, finally put paid to the religiophobes among his perceived critics? He sees no contradiction between self-understanding and quantum theory and, in conversation, eagerly shares the latest findings and postulates of physicists.

Whatever may be the ultimate nature of things (here merely suggested — metaphysics shaped into a visual — powerfully, elegantly and completely), for flesh that bleeds, a cosmos-badged and consuming behemoth consciously and indifferently bears it all forward ("His bones are like bars of iron" — *Job 40:18* — here made wispily airy). So it has been, so it is, and so it will be, whatever the changes that appear (as they surely will out of that star-specked, dark blue space), with passages of piercing light. The template is ultimately benign; the inescapable connectedness of things shown as linked in afore-mentioned ballet-mode. A book he recommends at the time is Gary Zukav's *Dancing Wu Li Masters: An Overview of the New Physics.*

***

More and more Taylor's attention turns to the effect of worldly events and conditions upon the creative being and finally upon human awareness and perception itself. He introduces recognizable figures usually within an imagined or transported context with the aim of having the one comment upon the other and to arouse inquiry and debate and reflection within the viewer. The suggestion, indeed the declaration is always of a heightened or "visionary" reality that, not unlike Plato's cave-dwellers, the figures cannot see and that their choices deny to them.

The shift in the initial painting, *We Know Not Where We Stand,* is toward the most egregious violations in the everyday world. He goes on eventually to destroy the result, unable, as he declares it, to stomach the interaction of the transcendent with the blood-soaked human ground. Hypersensitivity betrays him, and the world loses another *Guernica.*

Taylor pointedly follows this effort (while it still survives his compulsion to self-edit) with *Wounded Creature Flying Home* that requires no words to elucidate the sequence. It can stand on its own but,

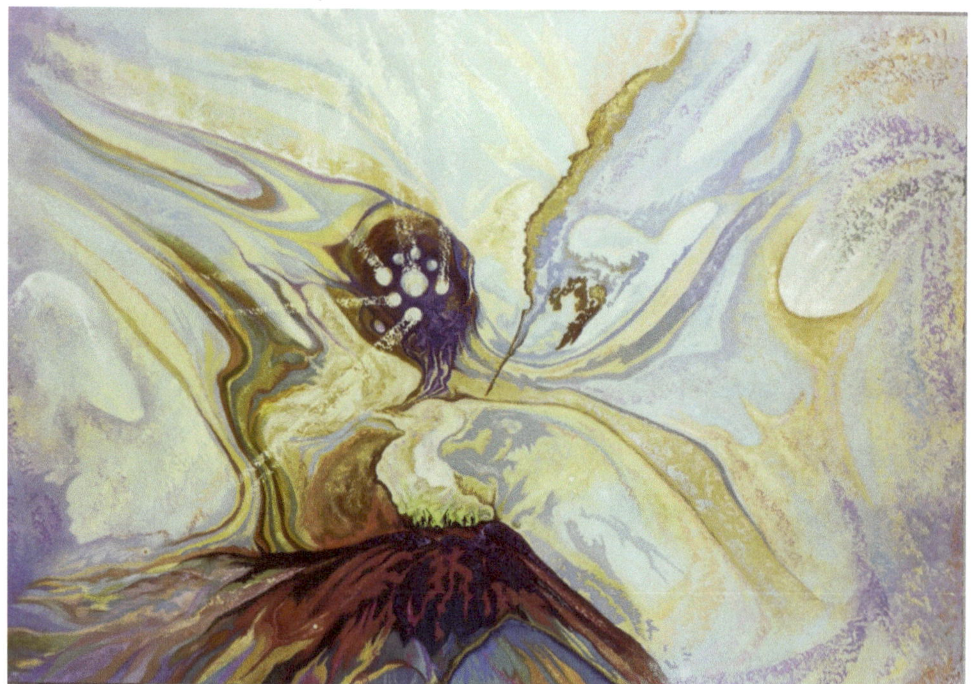

We Know Not Where We Stand, 1982 (painting destroyed by artist)

coming after the killing field of *We Know Not Where We Stand,* it exposes more surely the destroyed painting's connection to the vulnerable nature of the artist's communing spirit and presents another element
to the visual self-narrative and the change of focus to the human condition as he perceives it.

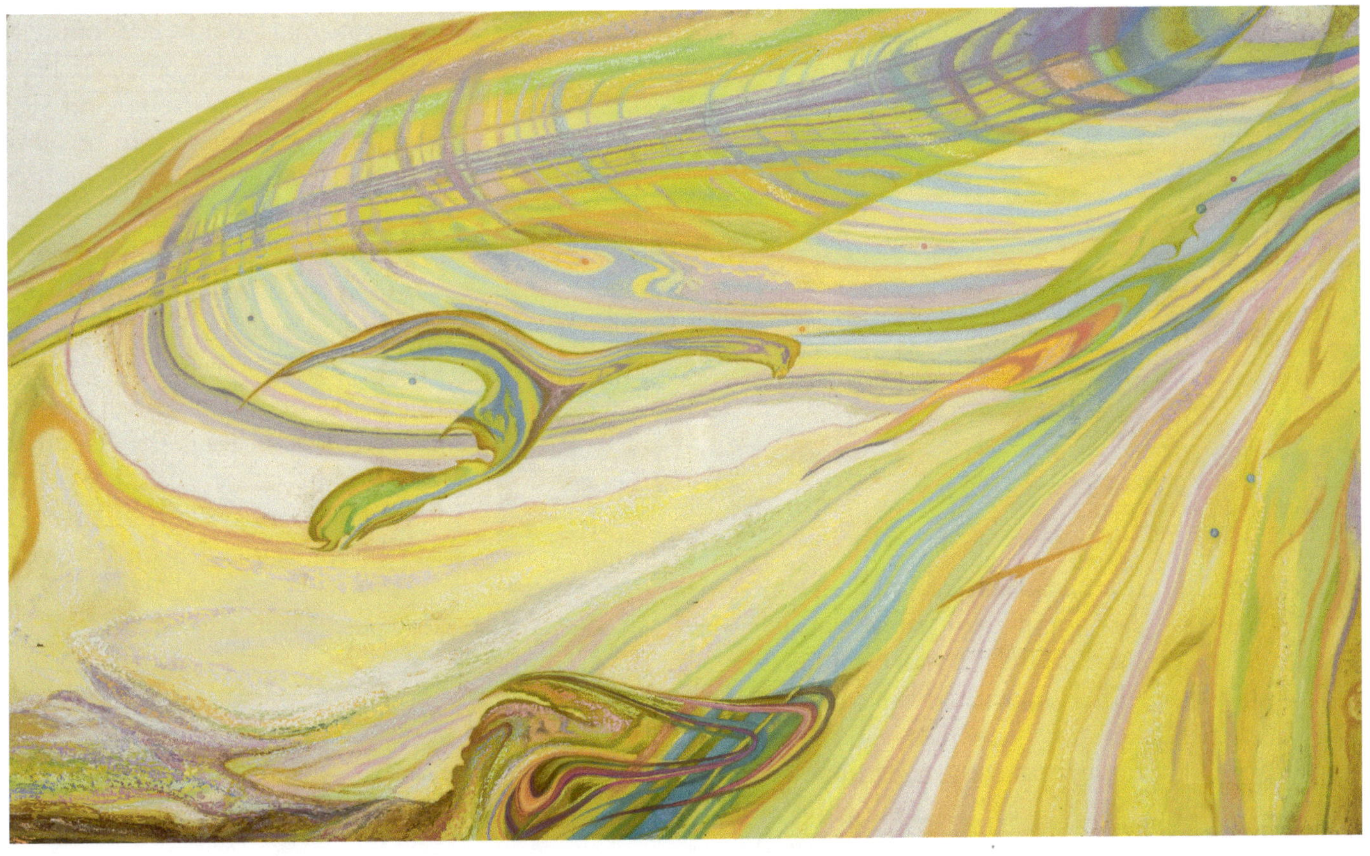

Wounded Creature Flying Home, 1984

The painting signals an end to one part of his narrative arc. Taylor ceases to explore and dwell
upon personal aesthetic identity as subject but, naturally enough, looks to its emergence through his
handling of his medium. He has taken it as far as he can in its relationship to the cosmos as a whole.
Whatever the triumphs for the aesthetic spirit that he has contemplated, consciousness must rise to it
through a visual critiquing of the surrounding immediate.

***

As if to prove just how impractical an artist can be, Taylor engages with his friend to produce a series of
rocking butterflies as an item whose uniqueness virtually guarantees it a market, so they speculate. Very suit-
able for "a Japanese prince," he remarks, not particularly considering how many of this type of persons the
world contains. It is the design and creation of a rocking horse as Christmas present for his friend's niece that
inspires them or sets their minds riding off in this fashion. Tied to the top of the car, it makes quite a show on
the highway from Toronto to Montreal. In their later discussions, as they mull over their futures and how liberating it would be to be able to paint, in the one case, and write, in the other, full time, they conceive a plan
that should enable them to do just that, they conclude. Unlike with the paintings that he wishes to keep together, Taylor doesn't at all mind flogging artfully produced butterflies.

He has already taken one sabbatical in order to have an unbroken period for painting that lasted for

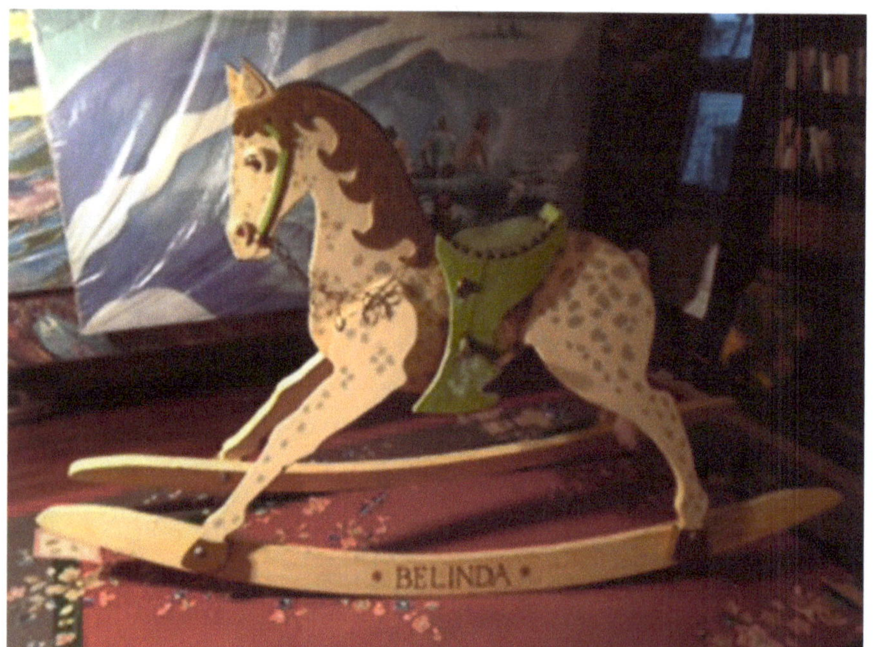

well over a year, with the two summers included in the package. The amount he accomplishes has him yearning never to have to return to the classroom. (He now has tenure at Concordia.) He takes another leave that lasts two years, the second year unpaid. Winter finds them at work on their planned fifteen rocking butterflies, barely warmed in the frost-rimed studio either by the wood stove or by their labours on the lathed bodies and huge wings. They have metal rockers made and, at first, the butterflies are meant to have small saddles and stirrups so that the Japanese prince and his cohorts can ride them. Soon disenchanted with a task beneath his capacities, Taylor comfort-

ably adopts the role of an old Master delegating and instructing his apprentice, paint-challenged friend as to the basic laying in and harmonizing of the oil colours. After three pieces are completed, they decide it makes more sense to forego the rockers, stirrups and saddles, paint the creatures on one side rather than two and have the result hang on a wall. Should their efforts galvanize the art world, one thing will lead to another, and they will proceed with their pockets full and be able to provide for what really interests them.

The following summer, with fifteen works in hand, a gallery on Queen Street is willing to show a selection for two weeks in its front window. (Other galleries pronounce upon the "beauty" of the offerings while excusing themselves due to the expectations of their established clientele. "They are so gorgeous but, no, we really couldn't take them.") With few regrets the enterprise ends there. Over the years, Taylor's indifference or absentmindedness leaves many of these butterfly creations under skylight leaks, or his overfull studio causes him to stumble into them, so that few survive. Taylor spends the remainder of his sabbatical on his own paintings and, at the same time, arrives at a conclusion: one more year — two terms — of teaching under his belt and he can take early retirement. He considers the reduced income but, at the age of 55, determines to go ahead.

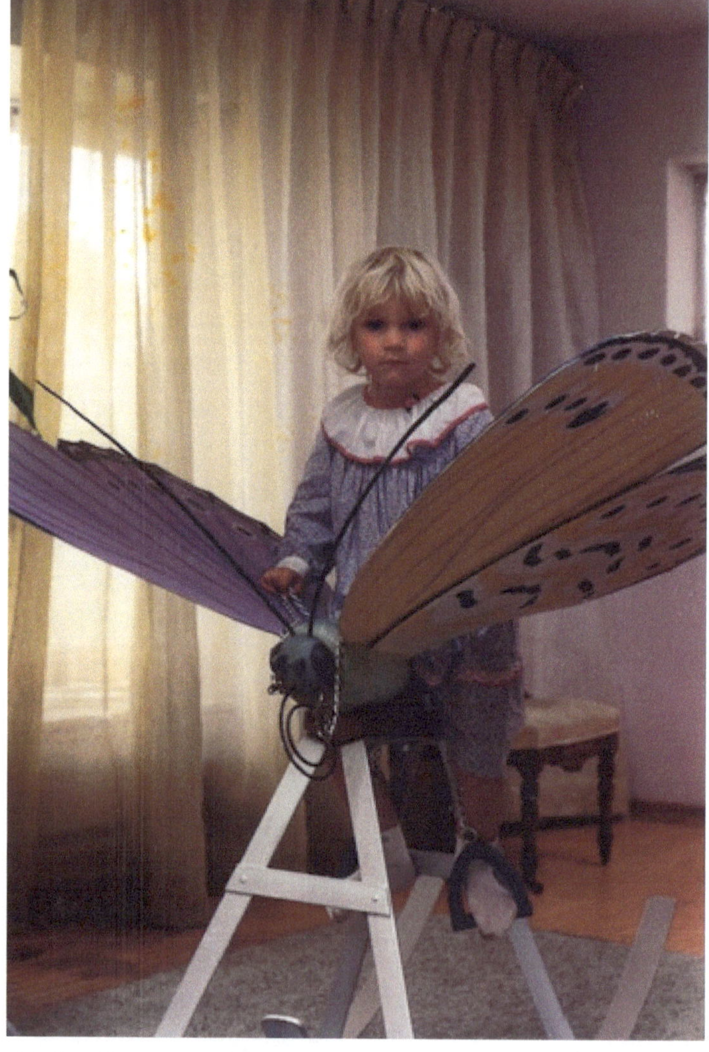

(Gabrielle, niece of the artist's friend, on a rocking butterfly)

CHAPTER II

The Visionary Figurative

It is either as a university student or during his first lectureship at Huron College, University of Western Ontario that Taylor takes lessons in "the noble art of fencing." His succeeding paintings after *Wounded Creature Flying Home* respond to the immediate world as it variously strikes him with a rapier aesthetic. A canoe trip — one of many — finds the painter on familiar, and yet instructive territory. "How, On That Little Map, May You Find Your Place?" he whimsically writes on the lower left canvas.

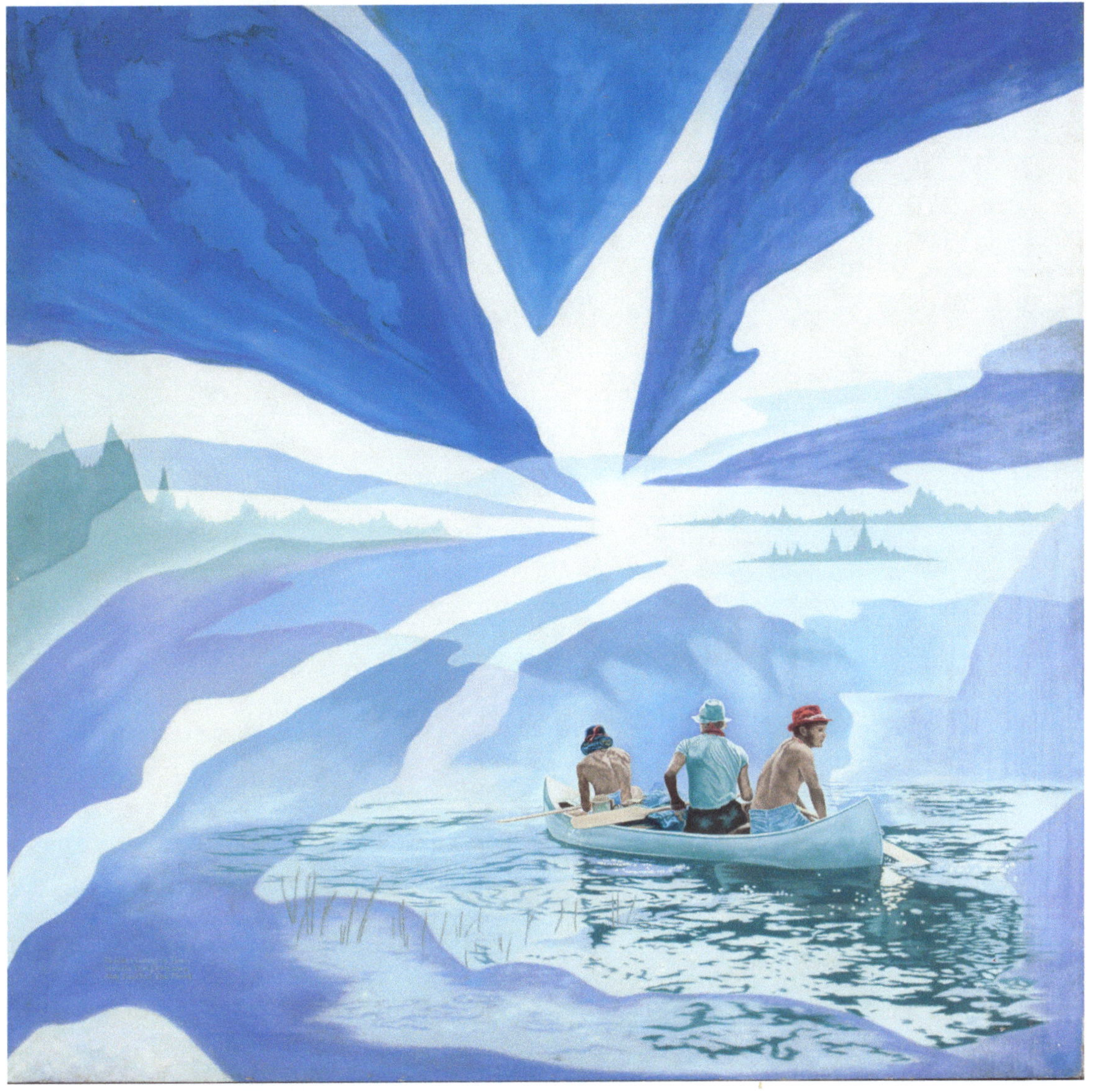

Paddler Floating in Time, 1984

Patently unaware of their true life's destination and oblivious of anything beyond the most immediate circumstance, three young men look to find a sign of what is to be their way. Should they attune themselves to and consult the greater import of the moment — existence itself? — this would transform what comes of their choices. Similar questions, similar observations guide the viewer in paintings to come.

The subject of human disconnectedness to a world beyond humanity's own making intrigues Taylor. Combining the two allows the artist to critique the one without losing sight of what awaits human potential — Blake's "timeless realm of Beulah" whose nature, as a graduate student, he debates with Northrop Frye.[33] When the man-made becomes more and more indispensable, the danger is that all else merely serves human ends and its fuller significance fades into greater non-existence. The irony follows that the natural world is no longer available to the fabricated social personality for all its gains beyond a perilous dependency.

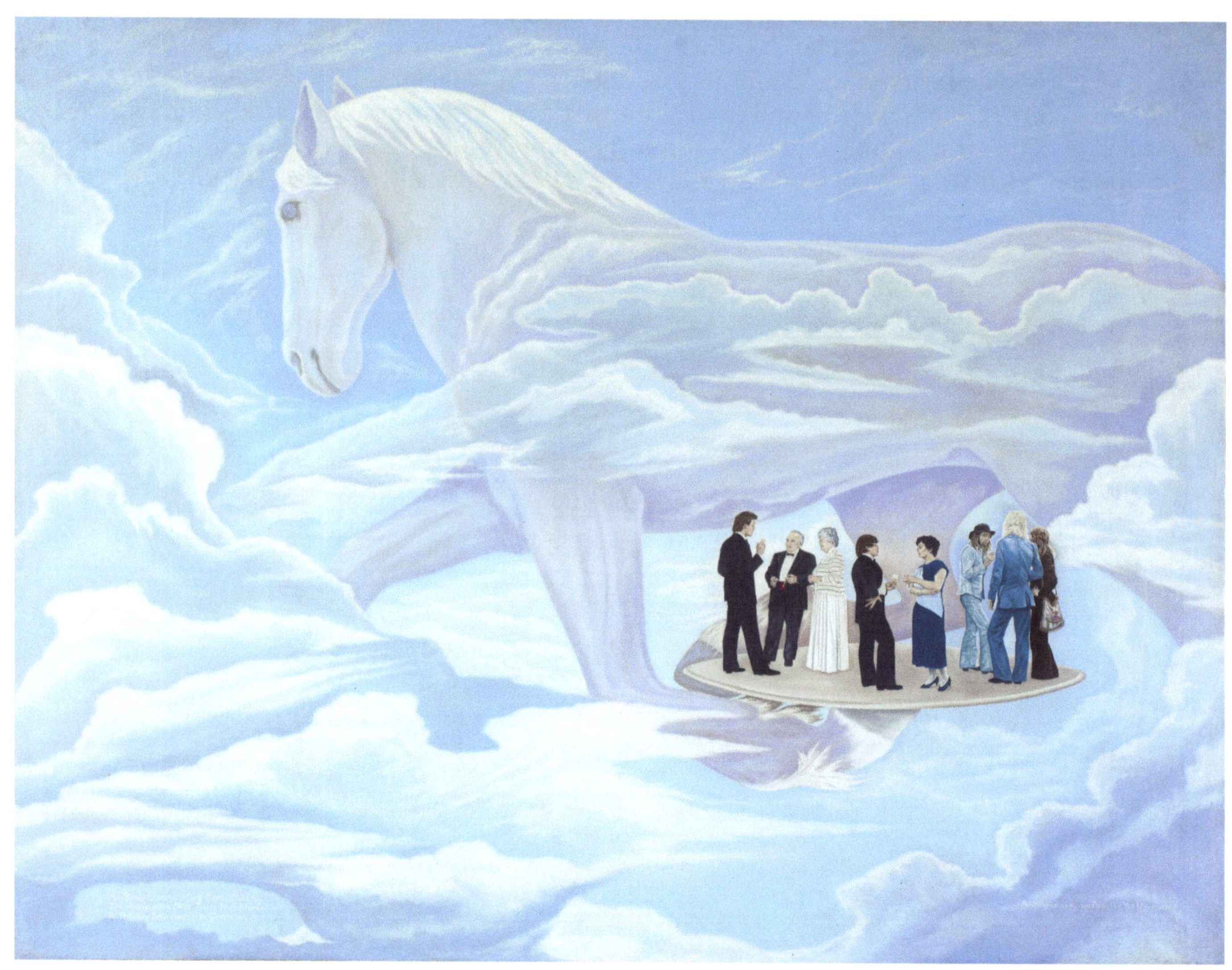

The Assumption That There Is A Horse, 1986

Inscription front left side:

"As People Become More Sophisticated,
The Assumption That There Is A Horse
Will Grow Less And Less Common."

---

[33] Taylor, *The Winnowed Field*, 136.

Sophistication rules in consciousness uninformed of what sustains its shrunken orb. The model for the central figure is the painter himself, the rest of the cast drawn from neighbours and acquaintances as well as hipsters, oblivious to his pointed camera in London's Trafalgar Square.

The Economist, November 17–23, 2018, edition, writes of present day society ("Living the Dream, The prophetic art of Andy Warhol") how the consumer has become a form of artist identifying the self with every purchase and entertainment, in a continual process of renewal and reinvention:

> "From his [Warhol's] perspective, people seemed to have no fixed centre; they were merely bundles of urges that changed in response to the latest come-on, their appetites always primed but never sated. They were defined by what they bought, the shows they watched, the clothes they wore — all of which were disposable."

The ultimate sophistication is to be disposable, to assume that one's self does not, in fact, exist.

As with Blake, organized religion is anathema to Taylor. It inevitably brings conflict, contradiction and chaos, and inflexible paradigms that militate against the inquiring spirit.

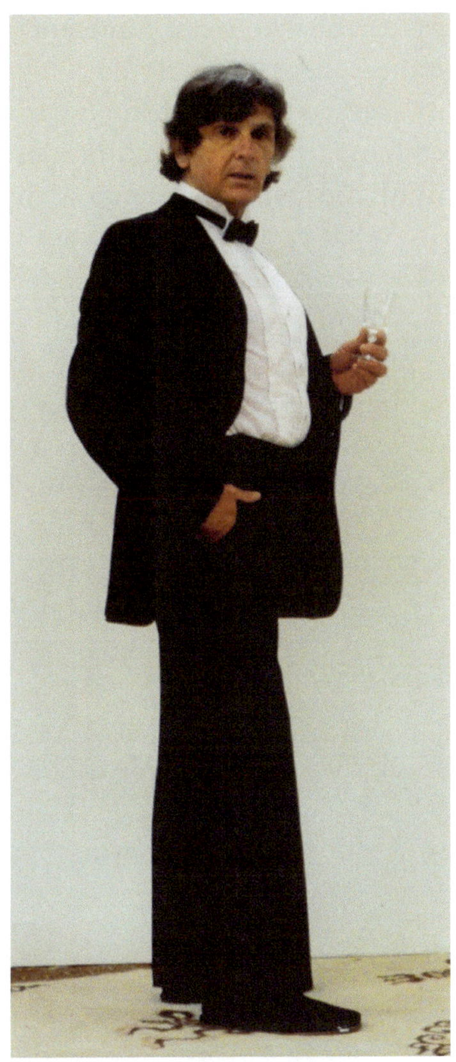

The artist poses for his painting

< *Phantasmagoria,* 1987

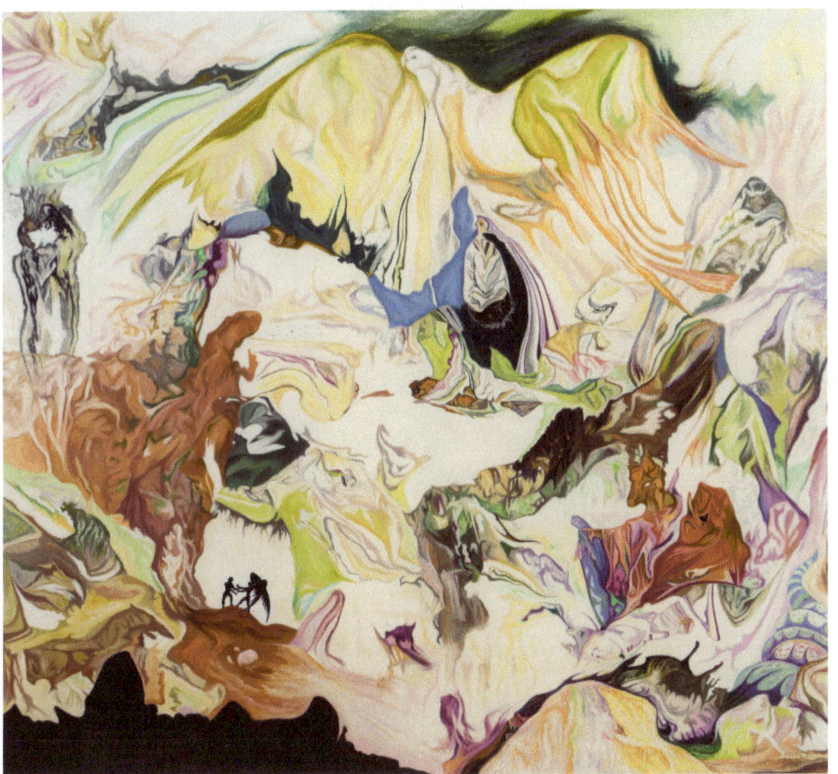

In *Phantasmagoria*, an angel (lower left) struggles to draw Everyman into the ecclesiastical power game and its shabby hierarchy, the spirit of it all a pillar of ashen smoke (upper left) rising behind a molten pastoral figure of lava origin admonishing a pink-puckered, meretricious creature homing in on the nether regions of a feline Satan, triumphant paw thrust upward (centre right). In the bottom left, a rear view of a helmeted entity observes the unfolding scene as does a coiled, antennae-at-the-ready mollusc — part of the proceedings — to its right. The whole cast is present: a feather-bare, giant-of-a-dove church hovering in imminent proscenium collapse over all the witchcraft; a blue-clad Madonna under the sway and encouragement of a red-garbed bull (re-emerging in a future Minotaur painting *Recapitulation*), and a cardinal's red-sheeted lump of malevolence, proboscis vertical (all bottom quarter right). Revelation has frozen over beneath the snow-clad slopes (right, beneath church's wing).

What can be the result but for a sophisticated mankind to be adrift and perilously sited to work out its own salvation in the face of an apparently complete disconnection (*The Assumption That There Is A Horse*)?

Sic transit gloria mundi. The artist again appropriates his person to do service as tuxedoed model, filling out the crowd adrift in an orb-become-inflated-lifeboat, the former neglected and distant world of *The Assumption That There Is A Horse* now an all-too-real flat sea and advancing, orchestrating dark blue cloud synonymous in tone with background butte formation.

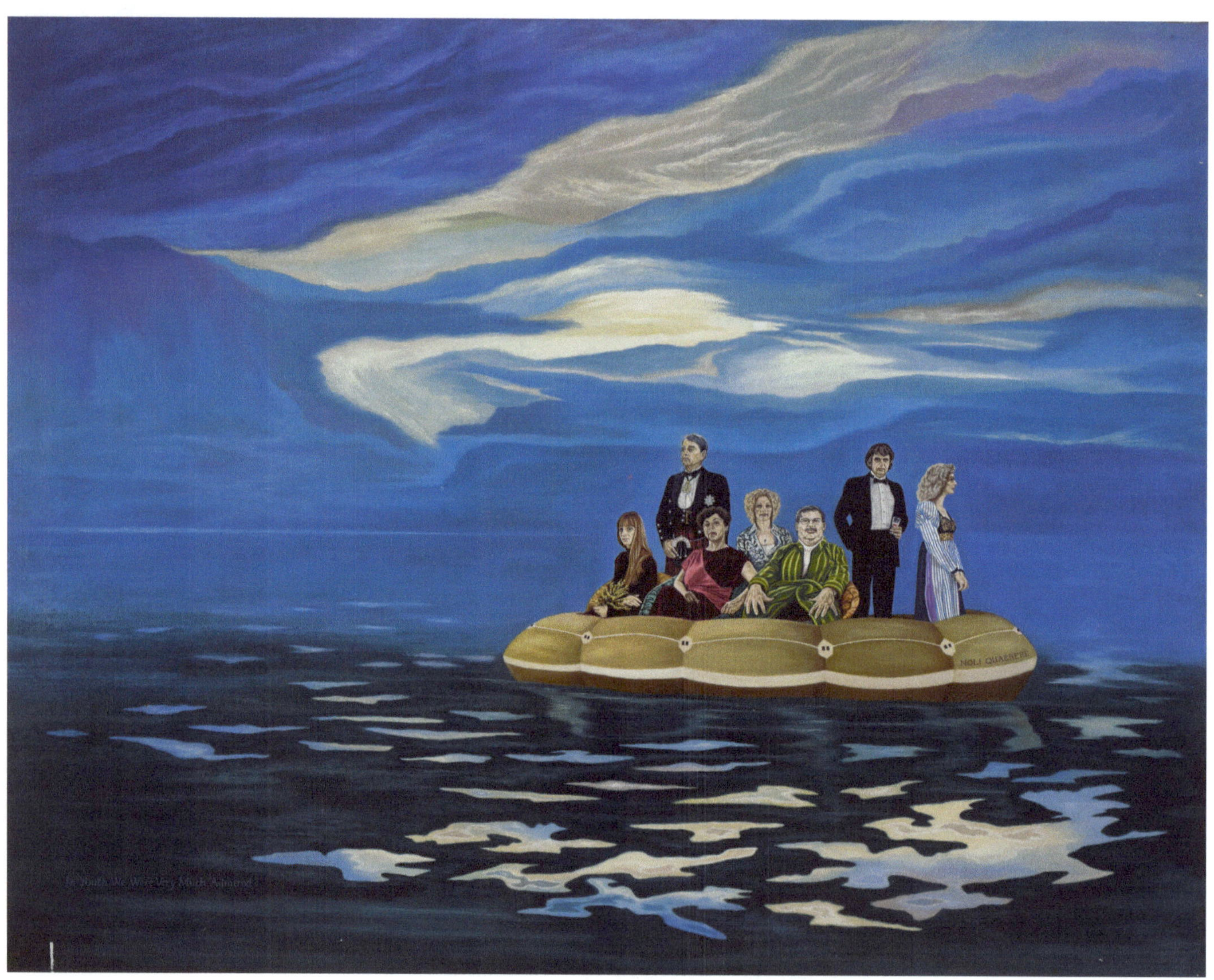

In Youth We Were Very Much Admired, 1986

In contrast to the *Assumption* painting, each passenger focuses too late outwards for a rescue that seems not to come, both consciousness and emblems of identity intact, but diminished and ineffectual.

Increasingly, Taylor critiques humanity's self-absorption and the constricted world it

delivers. Rightful self-definition requires full capacities of vision, unavailable to the purely
"bottom-line" personality:

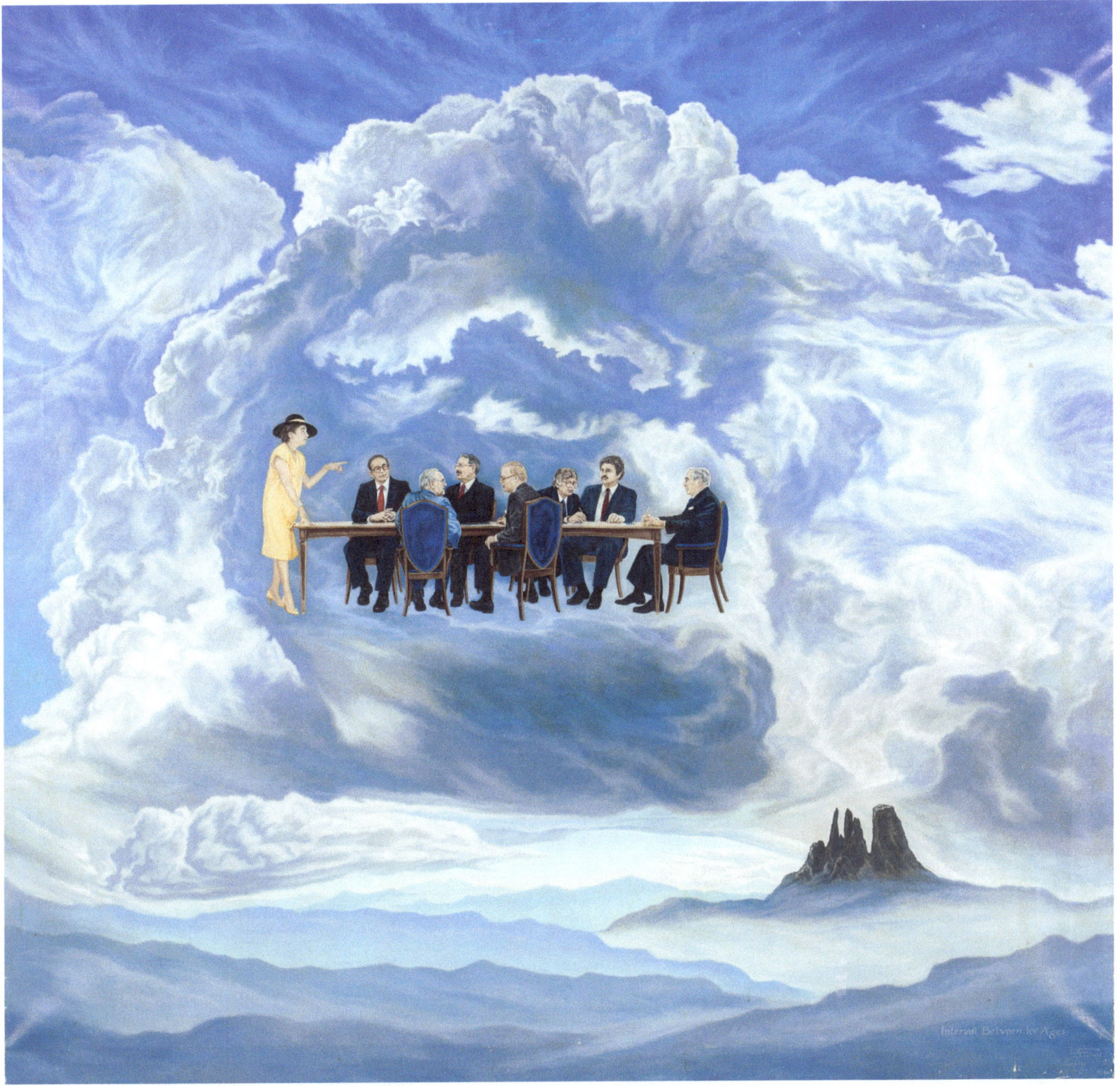

Interval Between Ice Ages, 1988

(The bent-over figure at the conference table would be Taylor, functioning as secretary.) The very
consciousness of finite existence argues, against all odds, for transcendent investments. How else o'er-
step the bounds?

Despite the worn-down, propped up narratives of history and tradition, the way to enlightenment
may be no more than a turn of the head away from the essentially mundane. Although it is little wonder that one can feel able to ignore questions of ultimate meaning when the immediately available answers are patently flawed human constructs.

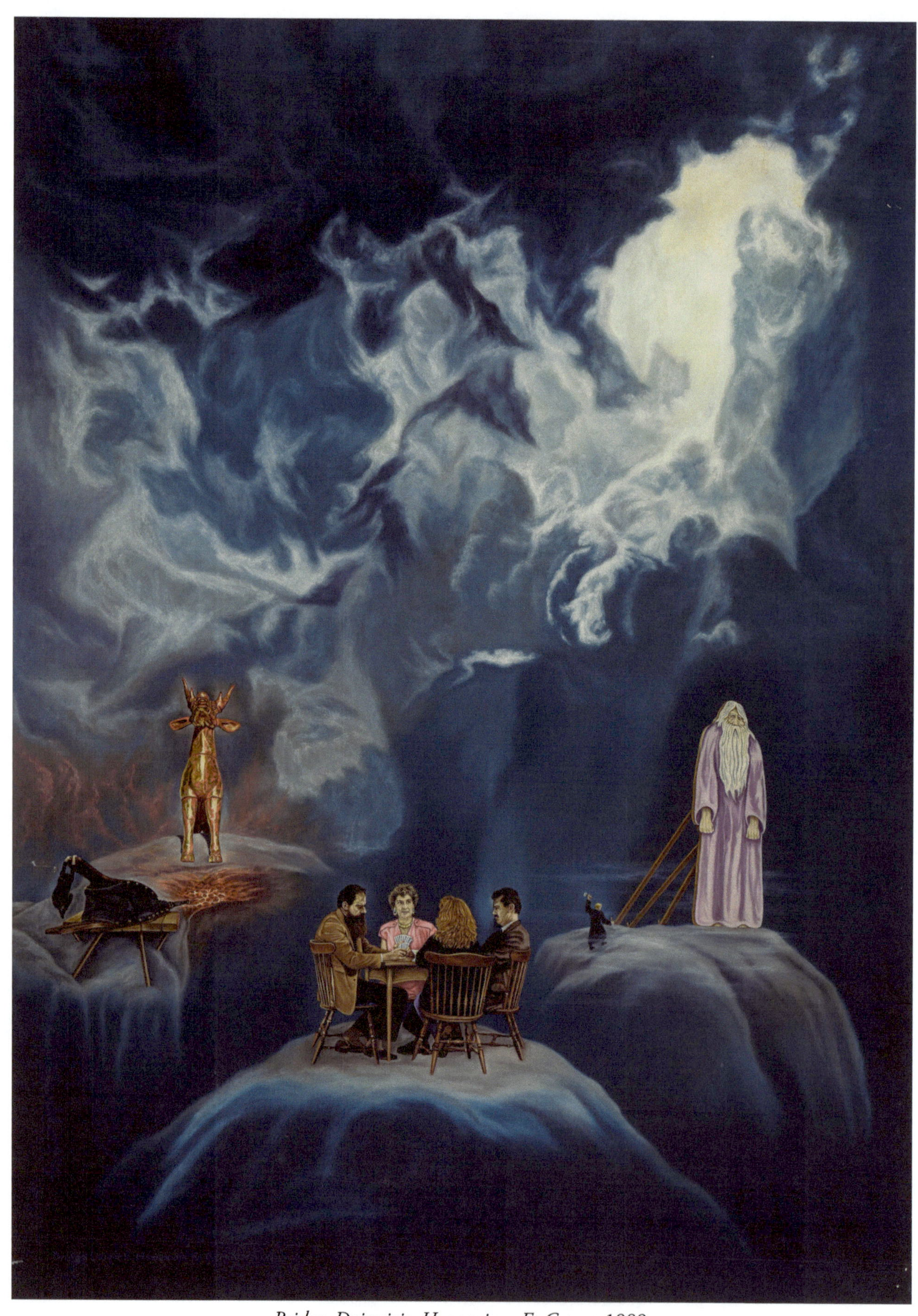

Bridge, Daiquiris, Humanism, Et Cetera, 1989

And yet, the issues remain as the very nature of things, having nothing to do with the manically fired up flames of hell and damnation or the redemptive capacities of a billboard deity. Heaven is not in the sky above, but something is, the above strives to proclaim.

Taylor has his friend pose naked. What makes him think of this and what is his purpose? Does he fear a self-destruction that he himself has known threatening the friend or does he have him stand as a surrogate for himself? Or something else entirely. What he does maintain, and powerfully, even corrosively experiences in his own life, is the connection between action and spiritual consequence or immediate effect upon sensibility and state of being. After all, he is someone who at one time walked away from the proffering of a surgeon's knife for the alleviation of what ailed him.

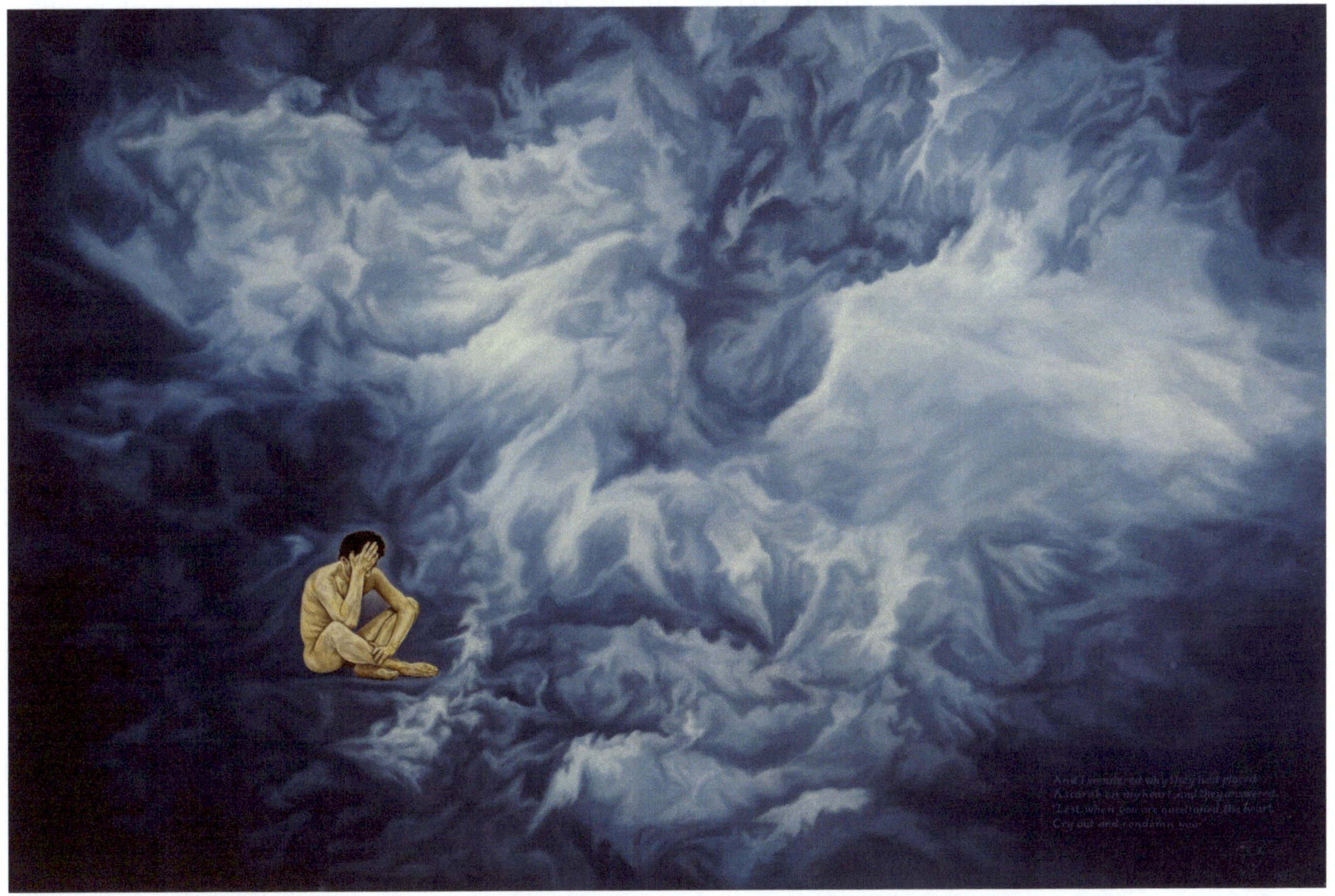

And All My Joys Are Sorrow, 1989

Inscription, bottom right:

And I wondered why they had placed
A scarab on my heart, and they answered,
"Lest, when you are questioned, the heart
Cry out and condemn you."

It would be obtuse in the extreme to take the easy convenience of Taylor's personal history as in any way the master key to unlocking his work, fierce observer and critic of the greater world that he was. He had if anything a tendency to dismiss the personal in himself and others when they presented as impediments to what truly counted. There is no need for an explanatory note pinned next to the painting on the gallery wall. What is of relevance is, rather, its posing of moral and existential questions in a manner that points to those inherent in the human condition. These universal issues operate upon the artist's sensitivities that, in turn, render them in high relief. The painting looks to responsive chords in the viewer without their being contingent upon knowledge of the creator's private life or, for that matter, the subject's.

In the biblical verse that provided inspiration for Taylor's *Angel, Revelations X*, the heavenly being has in hand a small book that when consumed is as sweet as honey and as bitter as gall. (*Revelation* 10:9 — "And he said unto me, 'Take it and eat it up, and it shall make thy belly bitter, but it shall be in thy mouth sweet as honey.'") Having to live with the debilities of his psychological make-up, comprised the gall for Taylor in the particular recipe for his life. His response to suggestions of chemical treatment was to quote Tennessee Williams: "If I got rid of my demons, I'd lose my angels."

Obsessive-compulsive and image-retentive to the point of debility he may have been, but he was nothing if not unfailingly civil and erudite when engaged with company. (Guests could expect cheese plates and wine, pastries and tea. They had no idea of the domestic preparations that their entertainment required from one who seemed to be alert to the appearance of his surroundings only when visitors were expected.) Disciplined to a fault before any sign of a falling away in his work, he applied all the meticulousness that he could bring to bear, and that astonished in its contrast to the cavalier disregard of everyday living conditions where he recognized a need for order — everything in its place — but little beyond that.

Instances of nature despoiled by human activity trigger rage. He repeatedly removes the surveyor's stakes intended to mark out a straightened course for the stream behind his house intended to alleviate flooding (caused, of course, by urbanization of what a few years before had been farm land). He comes upon such a violated landscape on a walk through Toronto's Rouge River Valley, a short car drive from his studio. Something more, however, acts upon his response.

Wind-Sown, 1990

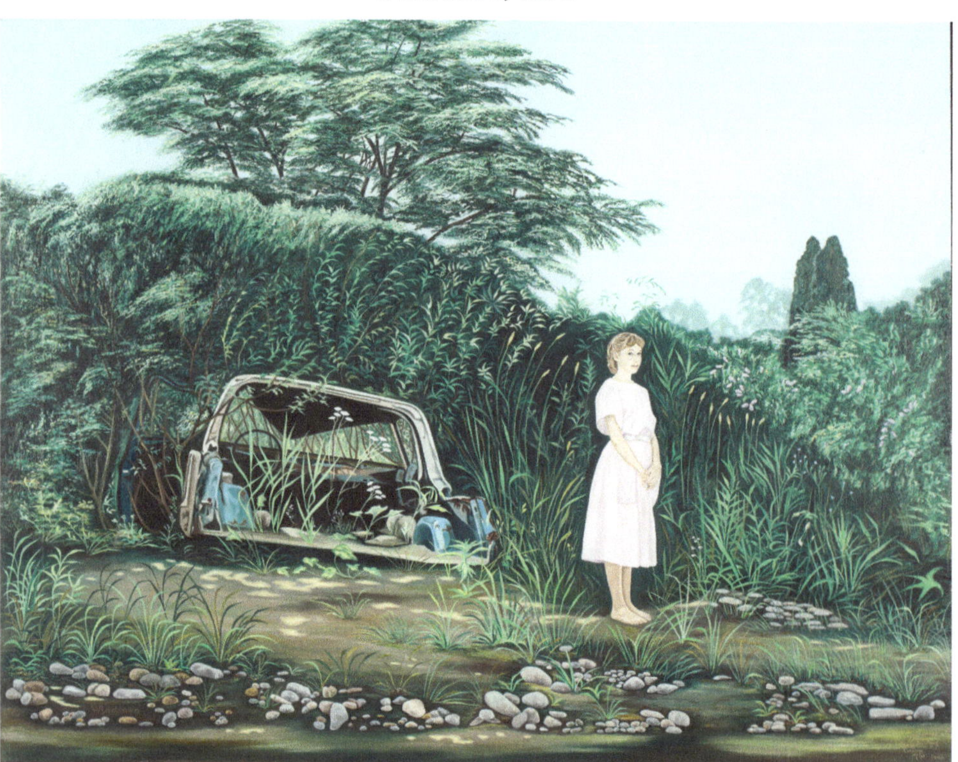

For all its painterly value, he would never consider for a subject of a canvas a lone pickup truck, dumped and gradually deteriorating in a natural setting, without the redemptive elements of life reasserting itself. Wild flowers work their way through the rusted-out truck bed, the wheels sinking into the ground. He poses, in all her purity and innocence, a Rousseauesque young girl in the scene, and its visibly diminished threat. Her representative person protects and confides the restorative, creative energies that lie deep within the heart of things, including humanity itself. Here, the visionary impulse and energies, so completely and rawly identified in renderings of aesthetic personality of the earlier paintings, he locates within the everyday, recognizable world. It is a harbinger of a near complete turn to the wilderness material that he gathers on yearly expeditions into the Algonquin, Quetico and Lady Evelyn Smoothwater River Provincial Parks.

A Time magazine article provides Taylor with the fodder to formulate a visual depiction of the disdain he entertains for much of the direction of 20th century modernism, in addition to venting over the horrors of this particular period in mankind's history. While not familiar with the full scope of the Scottish artist's work, the image presented to him of Eduardo Paolozzi gathering up "found" objects to incorporate into his art productions, strikes him as particularly ironic and, as a strategy, certainly both inadequate and pathetic as a response to the times.

His attitude to the canonization of similar practitioners follows a similar vein. The aesthetic sanctification of an artist's unmade bed with accompanying soiled detritus is all the justification he needs to accuse an art world of accepting the sorry excuse of "the dog ate my homework" for the homework and awarding the pupil an A. What could be more insultingly elitist than artists thrusting the everyday in the face of their fans with the claim that for thousands of years they have wrongly valued the muck of reality? Little wonder that the public turns away in disgust and bewilderment. Are there lines of visitors to gaze upon the 20th century's famous urinal, referenced still in hushed tones by the cognoscenti, the forerunner of future unmentionables that in a less gullible age would literally be flushed away in such a convenience?

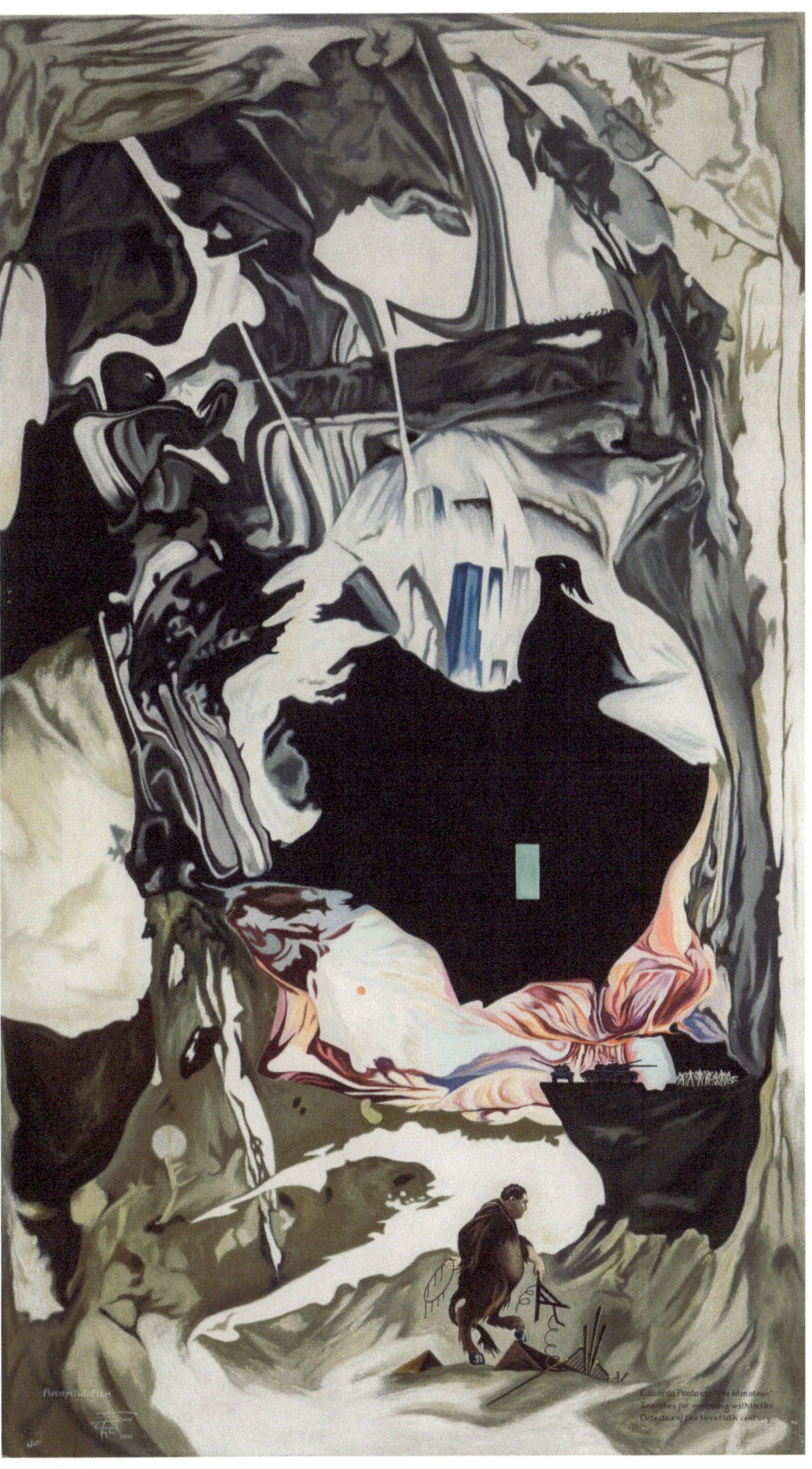

Recapitulation, 1990

It is easy enough to wake up in the morning and identify as artist if all it takes is one's authentic bed to legitimize the notion. Is some fundamental confusion operating between said artist's social and aesthetic personality, as Taylor identifies it, that infects those responsible for the venues that exhibit the "work"? And what can possibly justify the deplorable instance of the sale and purchase of an artist's packaged excrement, or that of his soiled undergarments, as an item worthy to be preserved and, subsequently, contemplated?

On the front of the canvas, Taylor inscribes, "Eduardo Paolozzi, 'the Minotaur,' Searches for meaning within the Detritus of the twentieth century."

Darkness engulfs the world in this satire. Light itself has become an instrument of this darkness, barely able to reveal the horrors of the age. The sun is recessive; a rectangular portal shows the world to be man-made, man-destroyed and enclosed as within a cave; there is little promise of anything to be seen through the opening. Were there a platonic ideal, it would ironically be the human form long cast aside in complete retreat from a world of vision. The doleful artist figure in the foreground has reduced himself to hapless scrounging for the materials of his art with all possibilities of transcendence denied and erased. Even in his animal-human form, he is indigenous to his world, the so-called modern age of the 20th century, but the artist has devolved.

Of some pertinence in regard to this work appears, perhaps, to be this from Roger Fry:

> ". . . transmutation of the visual values of natural objects into plastic and spatial values is the great problem of most modern artists, since the majority of them take some actual coup d'oeil as their point of departure for plastic construction."[34]

If an artist says it's a work of art, then it must be a work of art as long, of course, as the artist in question enjoys a reputation. As to whether or not the work of an unrecognized artist has value in that it substantially increases the capacity to appreciate, well, that determination more often than not rests upon the monetary valuations assigned to the work over time. Then and only then do the appreciative capacities of the viewer come fully into play. In other words, a complete abdication of rendering timely judgment is operative. The phenomenon of an acclaimed artist submitting a work anonymously for consideration and having it rejected and then subsequently accepted upon resubmission under known authorship is familiar and should be scandalous for many reasons — consider alone the legion number of worthy, deserving workers in the field who remain neglected, their lives in many cases tragic.

Taylor is catholic in his dismissal of what he calls "made-up truth." For him most human constructs are little more than a convenience without any great value in comprehending ultimate truths. In one painting, he traces this anthropocentric bias to its primitive origins, with two hunter-like characters guarding the concept of Wednesday cast for all to see in obdurate statuary. Questioned on the matter of its reality, all would acknowledge the indisputable fact of it. The calendar tells them so.

---

[34] Roger Fry, *Transformations*, (New York), 42, as quoted in Taylor, "Aesthetic Theories of Roger Fry Reconsidered," 65.

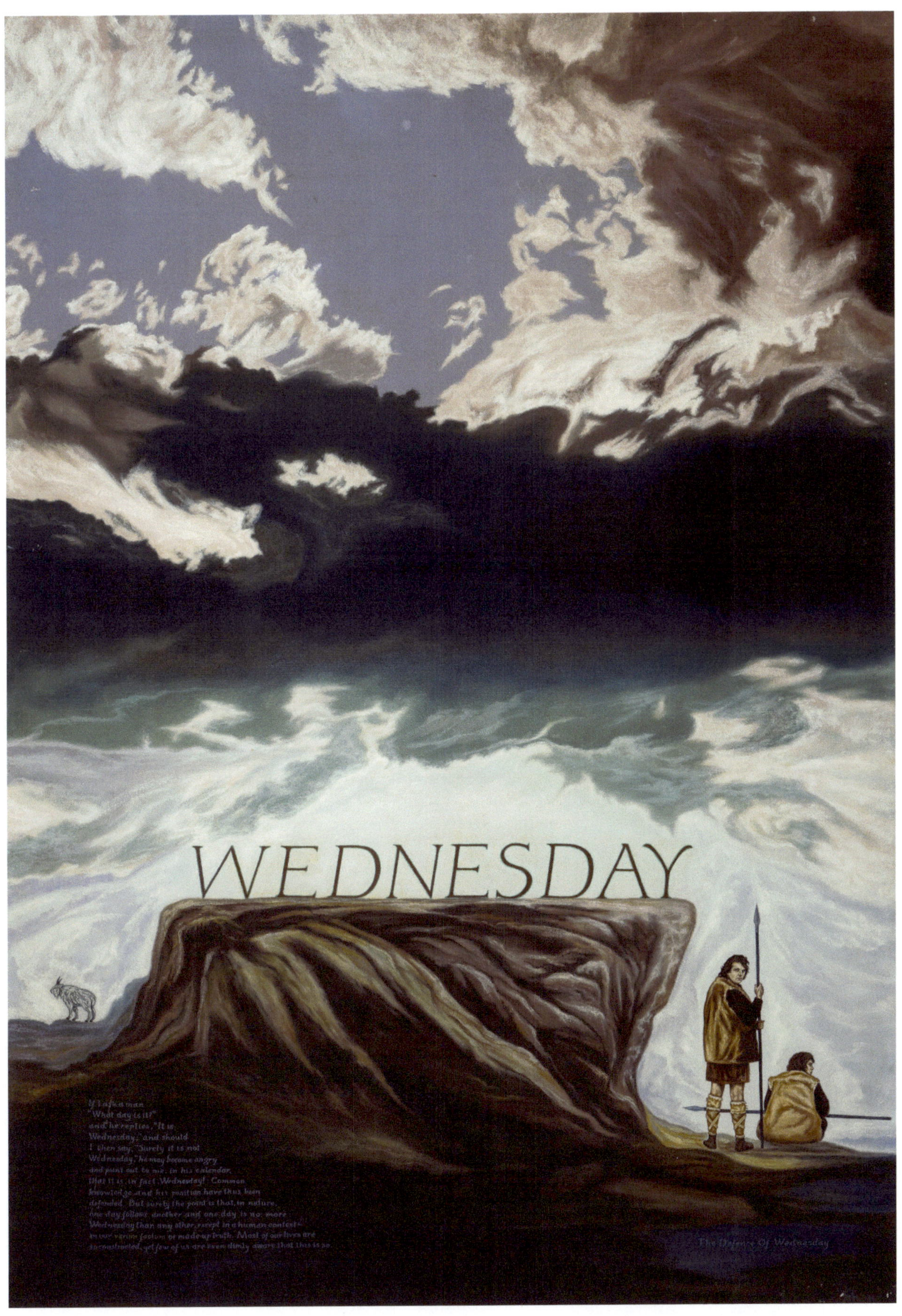

The Defence of Wednesday, 1991

The expansive sky has an atmosphere of patient tolerance for this ancient achievement, now accepted as reality, whose rendering in stark modern font separates its full meaning and implication from those who stoutly guard it. Taylor sees much of what is going on under the guise of art-making as a glorification of object and concept, and an inevitable, perhaps Soviet-type, triumphalism devoid of aesthetic substance as it infects the culture.

On the front of the canvas:

If I ask a man
"What day is it?"
and he replies, "It is Wednesday;" and should
I then say, "Surely it is not
Wednesday," he may become angry
and point out to me, in his calendar,
that it is, in fact, Wednesday! Common
knowledge and his position have thus been
defended. But surely the point is that, in nature,
one day follows another and one day is no more
Wednesday than any other, except in a human context –
in our verum factum or made-up truth. Most of our lives are
so constructed, yet few of us are even dimly aware that this is so.

CHAPTER III

David Taylor vs Francis Bacon
(The Visionary Figurative cont'd)

"I've always hoped to find another painter I could really talk to - somebody whose
qualities and sensibility I'd really believe in - who really tore my things to bits and
whose judgment I could really believe in."[35] — Francis Bacon

It is in a deconstructive capacity that David Taylor enters the list as a not at all tentative challenger to the
reputation of the putative "greatest" painter in recent memory.[36] The extent of the offence this artist took at
the paintings of his contemporary brought him to produce three works for its fullest expression: the *Francis
Bacon Triptych*. It should not be surprising to Bacon that his images would generate images in another visual
artist, having experienced similar occurrences when he confronted the works of fellow painters:

"Certain works ... have not only unlocked images for me, but also ways of thinking,
and even ways of behaving. ...They released something in me, and made way for something else. Let's say that it wasn't fruitless violence."[37]

The artist who was habitually scornful of traditional scholarly criticism might even have paid greater attention to and taken more personally than he usually did a critic who dared to meet him on the
same field of contest as it were.

However loaded with satire and social comment Taylor's paintings have been to this point, in com-
parison with what comes next, they count as a relatively civil and restrained critique of his contemporaries and society at large. His entire being bristles, however, when it comes to the figure in 20th century
painting who concentrates in his person and his work the nihilistic spirit that largely characterizes the
times and who unrelentingly endorses the darkness in man as the sole reality, an endorsement that largely
enjoys acclaim, acquiescence, or at least respectful tolerance in the art world. The extent of uncritical approbation and the buying frenzy that accompanies the sale of his work, if one sides with Taylor, suggests
that the artist has succeeded messiah-like in filling vessels that had been otherwise empty.[38]

---

[35] - In *Francis Bacon* as quoted by John Russell (Thames and Hudson, 1993), 178-179.

[36] See Daniel Farson, *The Gilded Gutter Life of Francis Bacon* (Pantheon Books, New York, 1993), 226-228, for the painter's hotly contested ranking.

Kenneth Clark identified Bacon as the "interpreter of our contemporary nightmare." As quoted in Michael Peppiatt, *Francis Bacon: Anatomy of an Enigma*, (Skyhorse Publishing, New York, 2009), 135.

[37] In Michel Archimbauld, *Francis Bacon In Conversation*, (Phaidon, 1993) 152.

[38] "A significant number ... were drawn to Bacon, quite simply, as a source of truth - an unvarnished truth of human ex-

In his published essays, Taylor argues for the existential reality of what he calls the artist's innate "aesthetic personality" that comes into play when he is at his work. The artist draws from a source distinct from his everyday social being when engaged in creative activities:

> "If [aesthetic] selfhood ... means anything, it would appear to approximate some characteristic principle of expression, whose emotional and expressive constituents may be seen to reside in the artist's medium, as he alone conceives it ... Such a characteristic principle of selectivity in the expressive resources of a medium would seem to find full expression only in the sensuously qualified statement of the artifact itself, since it is here that the artist's 'passionate colloquy' with his medium must take place or nowhere."[39]

Although his contemporary — Francis Bacon — from the many descriptions of his behaviour in the studio, in addition to his interviews, gives every evidence of a similar, not at all surprising disengagement from the social being, he appears not to have understood himself in the same terms and with Taylor's self-sufficiency:

> "[S]ometimes when I've been working I've been so sick of it that I just take the brush and put marks all over it, thinking it's not going to work at all, and then suddenly out of this chaos comes the possibility of making an image I hadn't thought of before."[40]

And,

> "[W]hen I work I only have a vague idea, sometimes even no idea at all of what I want to do. In a way it's purely by chance that something happens on the canvas."[41]

Taylor attributed an entirely different cause than the hazards of chance to his art. Again, reflecting on his signature painting *The Sounding of the Seventh Angel*, he wrote,

> "... the thing progresses, the original idea is abandoned, something else being dictated ... ."[42]

This personally emblematic work had established for Taylor the identity and authority of the creative being and it is this medium-based revelation that informed all of the work that followed. In contrast, the nihilistic nature of Bacon's self-identification proved to be the driving force of his own particular engagement with his medium and, as is widely understood, his vision and persistent denial of meaning as an artist.

The art critic Roger Fry's comments, appearing ten years before Bacon's *Three Studies for Figures*

---

istence that struck home with a force and immediacy which they had not encountered before, whether in art or religion. They haunted his shows in search of further revelation." — Peppiatt, *Francis Bacon: Anatomy of an Enigma*, 373-374.

[39] - David Taylor, *Aesthetic Personality*, 8. For further elucidation of his views, see also "The Aesthetic Theories of Roger Fry Reconsidered."

[40] - Francis Bacon as quoted in Farson, *The Gilded Gutter Life of Francis Bacon*, 86.

[41] Archimbaud, *Francis Bacon In Conversation*, 87.

[42] *The Winnowed Field*, op.cit.,146.

at the Base of a Crucifixion (1944), the artist's break-through work widely described as his *fons et origo* (source and origin), would have left the English painter unimpressed:

> "[To] face reality and probe deeper into its possible spiritual significance ... I believe to be the function of all the greatest art."[43]

Taylor's scholarship argues Fry's claim to be something not of otherworldly import, pointing rather to the direct and immediate experience of the artist at work:

> "Fry's use of the word spiritual … what is involved is essentially the operation of transmutative mind in the manifestations of sight, the bestowing upon these of the connotation of a distinct "spirituality," or sense of heightened visual and psychic activity."[44]

Bacon, for his part, entertains no possibilities of a transformative nature. The disillusion is complete:

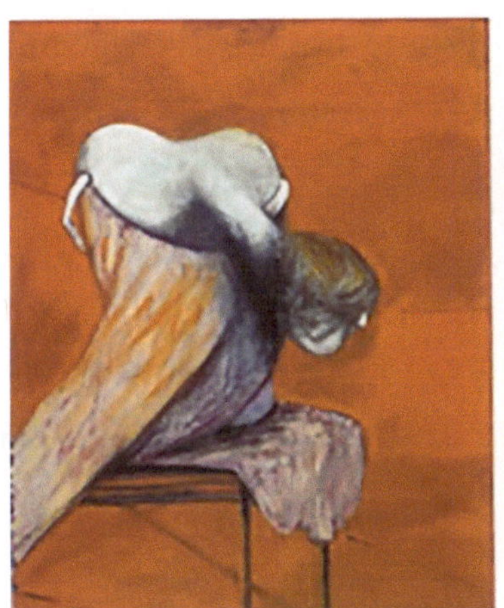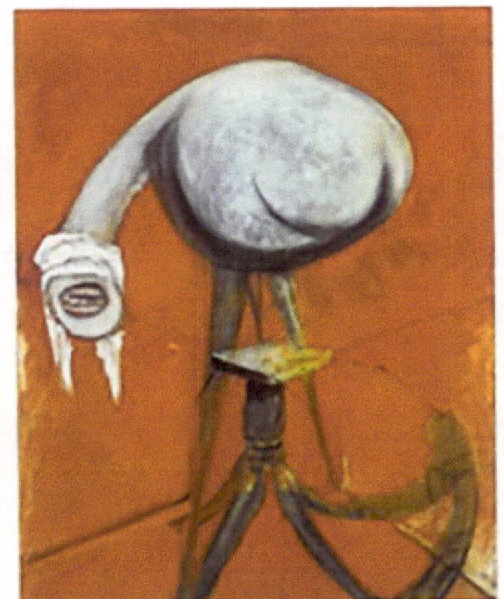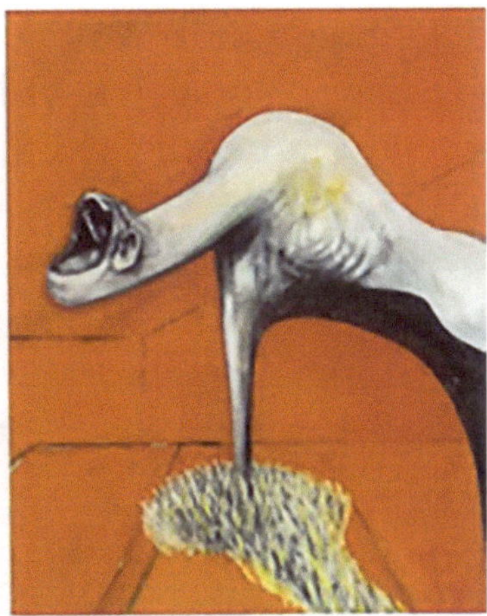

Three Studies for Figures at the Base of a Crucifixion, 1944

Bacon's "half-human, half-animal" ghoul-like figures — reminders of the creatures in our more recent *Alien* films — caused "total consternation" among the visitors to the gallery, some of whom "came out pretty fast."[45]

Viewers credulous of Bacon's premise that brutality is all have to rely on the response of their nervous systems to what is presented. ("Painting is the pattern of one's nervous system being projected on the canvas."[46]) Anything more would be unwarranted and illegitimate interpretation gleaned from the "gloss" (Bacon's word) of whatever distorting cultural, historical, moral lens one brings to bear.[47] How transcendent vision in whatever form emerges from brute composition or origins, he never seems to

---

⁴³ *Reflections on British Art,* 1934, as quoted in Taylor, *The Aesthetic Theories of Roger Fry Reconsidered,* p.70.
⁴⁴ Taylor, *The Aesthetic Theories of Roger Fry Reconsidered,* 65.
⁴⁵ ("[Three Studies] … an emblem of brute suffering, ravening greed and generalized evil." — Peppiatt, *Francis Bacon: Anatomy of an Enigma,* 105.
⁴⁶ Francis Bacon, *Time,* 21 November 1949.
⁴⁷ Michael Peppiatt, *Francis Bacon: Anatomy of an Enigma,* 154.

consider.[48] Where aesthetic identity or personality was innate for Taylor, Bacon would not have countenanced the assertion; somehow, for him, in a manner difficult to imagine, the artist's talent would have to issue from, or be the "gloss" upon a meaningless brutality.

Bacon returns to the same Crucifixion theme with similar treatments that contain a greater multitude of recognizable elements from and references to the traditional depictions, the human sacrifice for Bacon being the central message to "the greatest story ever told." It escapes him, perhaps as inconsequential, that even a purely secular view of life is not antithetical to and will include rebirth for the human spirit in the aftermath of tragedy.[49] However disingenuous Bacon's denials of any meaning whatsoever, his various parallel treatments of the Crucifixion ironically enough establish and cement the oxymoron of nihilistic meaning for the rest of his paintings.

When he does depict an actual full-blown *Crucifixion* (<u>Painting, 1946</u>, and the <u>Second Version ... 1971</u>), and not merely its horrifically realized attendants as in *Three Studies*, a butchered and splayed animal carcass represents the crucified figure in a clear "illustration" (an inescapable descriptive however much anathema to Bacon's declaimed aesthetic and his allergy to narrative element) of his view that life is as meaningless as meat (no more than meat coming into being).

> "His attitude to life, which deepened with time but did not alter, was based on an unyielding conviction of its futility. 'We come from nothing and go to nothing' was his most constant refrain and the bedrock of his belief."[50]

For Bacon, his reality is reality and the rest of us have merely to avail ourselves of his choice of lens, that is, the nervous system, to get on side:

> "'All I want to do,' he told me, 'is distort the reality of the human figure into reality'."[51]

Why Bring an Umbrella to the Crucifixion?

Why bring an umbrella to the Crucifixion if not to sneer at the fundamentalist take on an event that offers to the cynic, at most, an unnecessary soiling of one's person? Lesser minds respond in this manner to lesser minds, might be the critic's answer to the painter's strategy. The self-indulgence misses entirely the universal suffering that informs the Crucifixion. Would it have made a difference to Bacon had it been a loved one up there? Not, apparently, when considering his later exploitation of a lover's suicide.

---

[48] He appears to have been an autodidact, as far as that went, having had no formal education. Biographies of Bacon give the distinct impression of a cynical bon vivant with a nihilist champagne-fuelled schtick that his unprepared guests and drinking companions either submissively endorse or fail to readily answer. See, among other biographies, Daniel Farson, *The Gilded Gutter Life of Francis Bacon*. "Something he never ceased to say was: 'We are meat,' and then he would raise his champagne glass with that inimitable 'Cheerio!'" 141.

[49] A common enough human experience sufficiently significant to be the theme of Shakespeare's "romances" as his final plays — *Pericles, Cymbeline, A Winter's Tale, The Tempest* — are identified. Bacon, for his part, selectively appreciated only the tragedies, notably the blood-soaked Macbeth.

[50] Peppiatt, *Francis Bacon: Anatomy of an Enigma*, 159.

[51] Farson, *The Gilded Gutter Life of Francis Bacon*, 141.

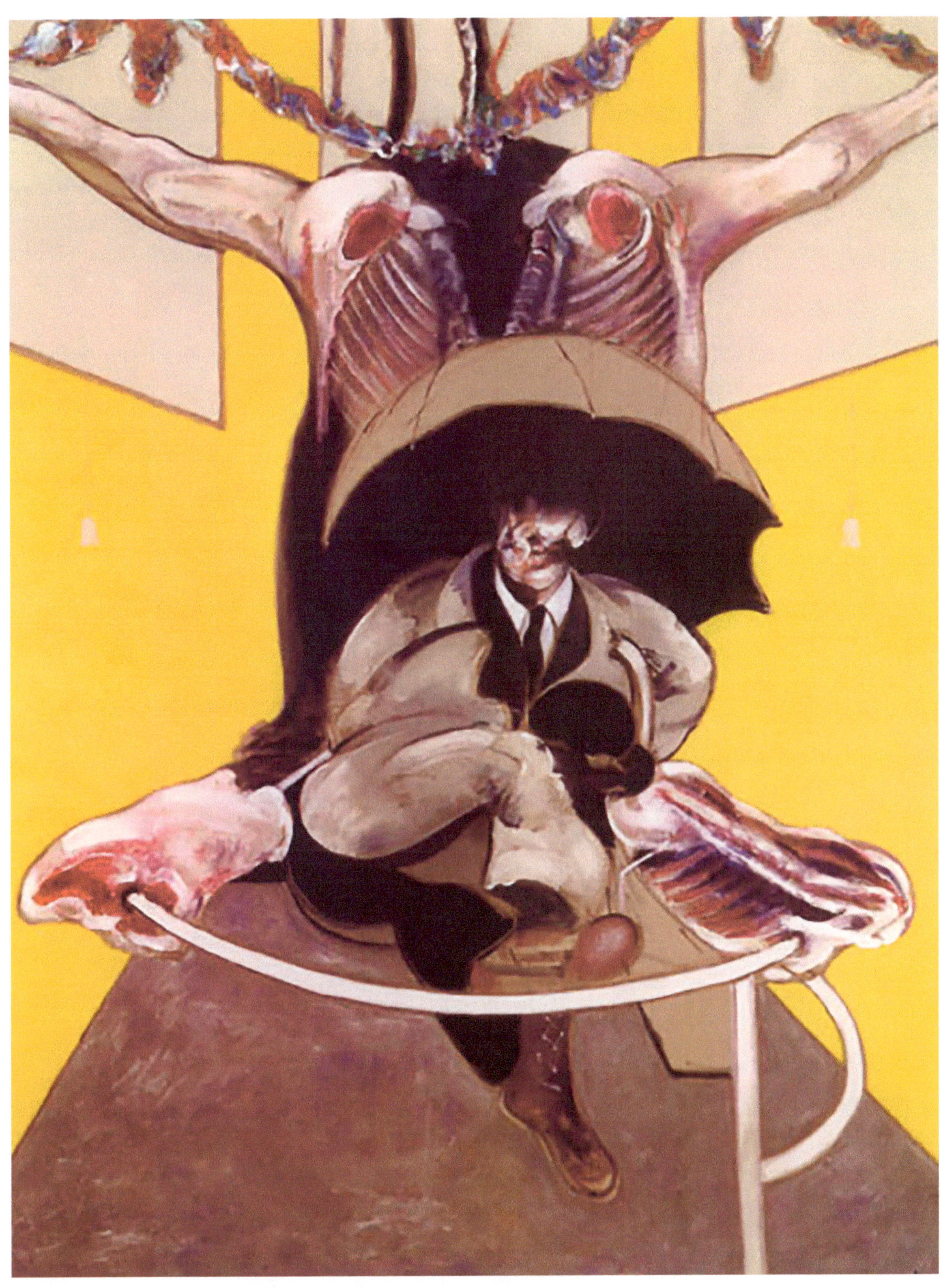

Second Version of (1971)

Two impaled joints of a carcass, possibly victims of lesser stature — thief and murderer in the original religious iconography — flank the foreground of the monstrous, proprietorial, possible deity figure posed to the front of the crucifixion and protected beneath an umbrella from — what else? — blood splatters in a retort to higher supernatural or metaphysical claims. Future paintings in the same mold continue in obsessive manner to utilize these images whose obvious narrative Bacon constitutionally resists, and yet his umbrella accessories undeniably participate in a personal reading of a story that rejects higher meaning ("We are meat") and yet contains its own. Their secular, sheltered arbiter expects blood and blood alone from brutality's dispensation and, especially at this occasion, a need for protective gear.

Bacon's crucifixions both deny and cancel the real "message" of the historical treatments that he draws upon:

> "It was this keen sense of the beast in man which also attracted Bacon to the Crucifixion as an elevated example of man's brutishness and as a theme which allowed him to conflate images of the abattoir with some of the greatest icons of Western art."[52]

That is his presumptive message:

> "When Jean Clair said of the right-hand panel in … *Three Studies for a Crucifixion* (1962) that it was 'almost a scene of slaughter, butchery, mutilated meat and flesh,' Bacon replied that 'Well, that's all the Crucifixion was, isn't it?'"[53]

Some may beg to differ:

> "*What is wrong with Francis Bacon?* He has not noticed that, halfway through, the Crucifixion turns into its opposite. Tintoretto noticed; so did Rembrandt; even Dali noticed."[54] [italics mine]

Bacon's nihilistic or self-cancelling "narrative" — despite all protestations, he cannot dispossess himself of the term — in fact sets the stage and initiates the informing spirit for the rest of his paintings despite the improbable disclaimers of meaning that he insists upon throughout his career. None of his paintings that came before his fons et origo interest him. He gives the distinct impression that his dismissal extends to most of the Western World's art canon, not excluding its music and literature although he had a fondness for tragedies, The Oresteia[55] among his favourites. He would selectively refer with similar approbation to Shakespeare's tragedies, ever singling out his bloody Scottish play, Macbeth, while neglecting all consideration of the playwright's entire body of work that culminated in the transcendent final Romances whose treatment of character ultimately sheds the lineaments of tragedy for the finer dress of what is redemptive. It is on the basis of his nihilism or spirit of denial that, as Russell writes, "nothing" that came after the fons et origo would "ever be the same."

---

⁵² *Francis Bacon: Anatomy of an Enigma*, 74.
⁵³ Ibid, 193.
⁵⁴ Bernard Levin, *Time*, 28 June 1985.
⁵⁵ Aeschylus. The Greek tragedian's line "the reek of human blood smiles out at me" (*Eumenides*, 253), an intellectual touchstone for Bacon, became critics' much-cited encapsulation for his view of life.

Bacon invests the subject matter that follows his Crucifixion paintings — subject matter that is, with one or two negligible exceptions, invariably the human figure — with the same sense of things:

> "Bacon concentrated on [what] was to preoccupy him for the rest of his life: the human figure in extremis - crucified, X-rayed, in flight, abandoned."[56]

More than one critic has noted how Bacon manages to turn his nihilism into a personal theology and certainly his psychological figurations show clearly as "contorted" spirits or beings:

> "The initial donnée in these portrait-heads is not so much distorted as contorted."[57]

This would also be the preferred descriptive of the artist.[58]

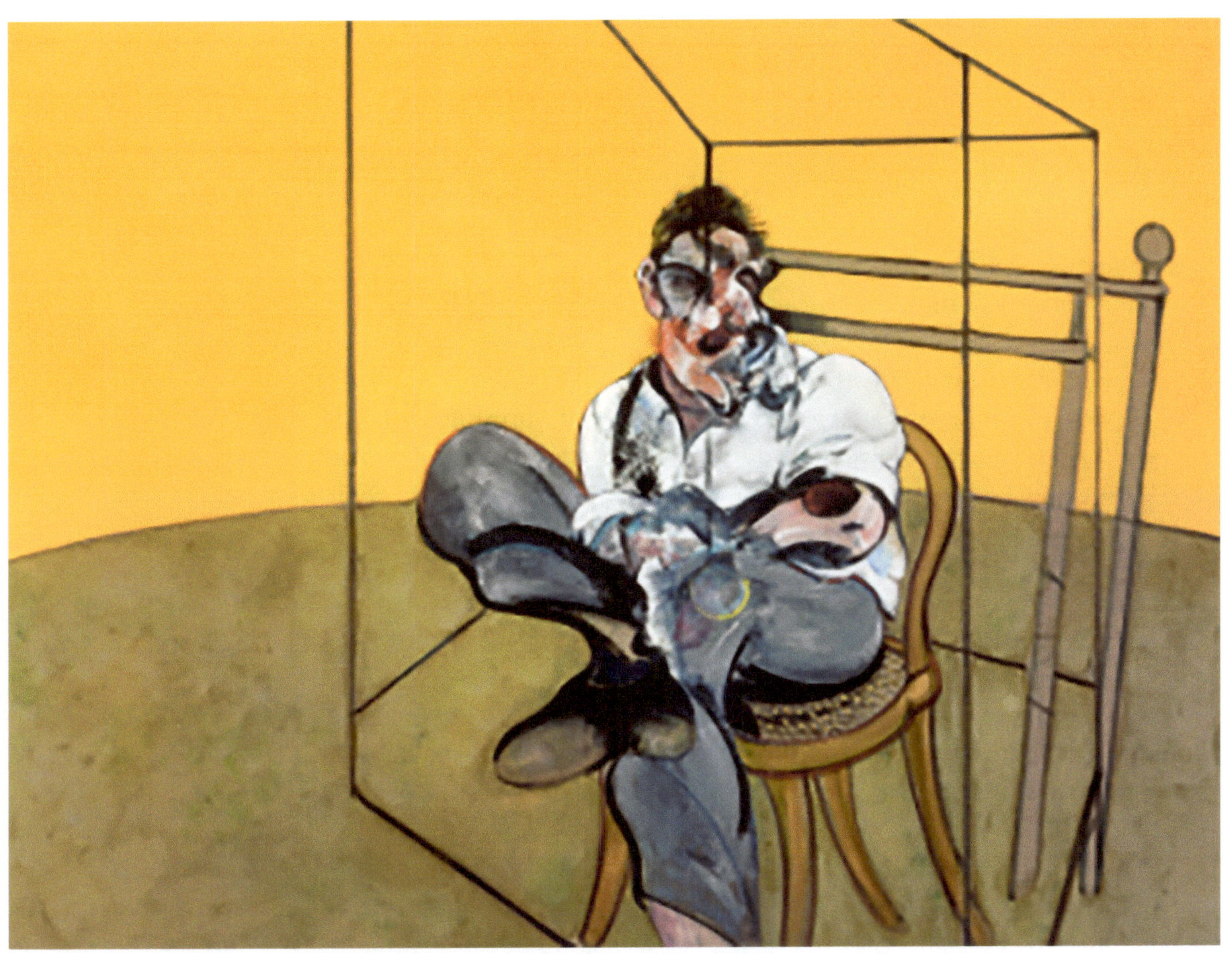

Central panel of *Three Studies of Lucan Freud*, 1969
(The representation of a bed's bare headboard suggests the condition of containment to be permanent.
One of countless Bacon paintings of this type. Taylor, for his part, never repeats himself.)

---

[56] *Francis Bacon: Anatomy of an Enigma*, 71.
[57] Ibid, 100.
[58] Michel Archimbauld, *Francis Bacon In Conversation*.

Whatever the life strategies and inner resources of those who "sat" for him, Bacon places his subjects in the grip of a void that mirrors his own sense of reality and presents these renderings of visceral sensation as a type of possession. When questioned, he dismissively refers to the broader range of human emotion as merely "the other side of the shadow." Life has no meaning ("Nada, nada!" as he was wont to repeat), and the most that could be expected of the artist was to communicate the fact or, at best, to communicate the bare-bones meaning that he births for himself:

> "We come from nothing and go into nothing, and in the brief interlude we might try to give existence a direction through our drives. But there's nothing. Nada. Do you understand? *Nada*." [59]

Or, he might say, for the whole of art preceding him, "Avant moi, l'illusion," in a denial of the past that seems to have infected much of modern art.

Francis Bacon is both target and foil in the three Taylor paintings that comprise the triptych bearing his name and that deliver the full scope of the artist's rebuttal. With relentless deconstruction, he addresses Bacon's persona as much as his art; the judgement is incendiary and challenging, the intensity both Goya- and Picasso-like, with singular prosecution of the case against the perceived moral failures of one who enlisted in, rather than critiqued, the spirit of a time that produced serial genocide, environmental devastation and nuclear holocaust:

> "When I told him [Bacon] about a brief television documentary in which, interspersed with newsreel clips of Hitler, Belsen and Hiroshima, the critic stood in front of a Bacon painting and explained to the viewer that it represented the artist's condemnation of man's inhumanity to man, Francis expressed surprise: 'Well, he would say that, wouldn't he? That's the last thing I think of.'" [60]

Taylor's indictments inevitably take on the character of one-sided polemics. In conversation, he goes so far as to dismiss out of hand the possibility of assigning aesthetic value to the painter's work separate from the disqualifying nature in his view of the subject matter. Rightly or wrongly, he brooks no position other than that a work of art is to be evaluated as a whole and is unworthy of endorsement should it fail in one essential aspect or another. The exploitation of a friend's suicide for visual rewards, in addition to its occurrence in embarrassing circumstances, is unspeakable, immediately disqualifying, and speaks to all the subject matter that preceded it.

Perhaps it is easier to entertain this absolutist view if one considers the notion of listening to music that is intended to communicate the composer's musical depiction of a lover's suicide upon a toilet as is the case with Bacon. (One can only appeal to Freud — perhaps he bears some responsibility — for the 20th century art world's obsession with toiletry and matters fecal. Think as well of Dali and his rendition of adults who had failed at basic toilet training.) For Taylor, content fatally undermines stylistic achievement.

---

[59] The painter as quoted in Peppiatt, *Francis Bacon: Anatomy of an Enigma*, 271.
[60] Farson, *The Gilded Gutter Life of Francis Bacon*, 137.

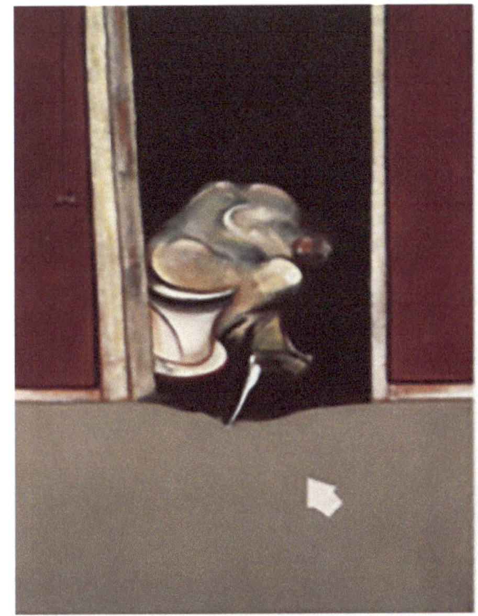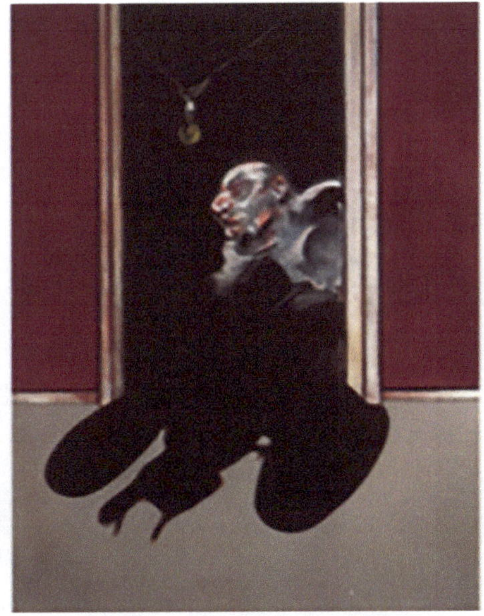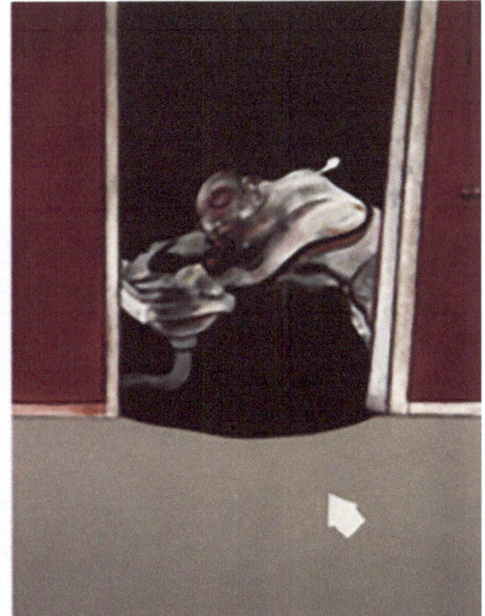

Triptych, May—June 1973[61]

Bacon's self-appraisal, even in later life, where he claims not to know what he intended beyond the purpose of "exciting" himself, as he began each new work, cannot help but give pause both here and in his earlier Crucifixion paintings:

> "[W]hen he said that he 'painted to excite himself,' he surely meant ... that, at one level
> or another, much of what he painted is a projection of sadomasochistic practices ..."[62]

See also *The Gilded Gutter Life of Francis Bacon*: "I paint to try and excite myself, which doesn't often happen."[63]

Unlike some who mirrored Bacon's own confusion as to the appropriate distinction between pleasure and pain, art and horror, Taylor is, in fact, especially incensed by Bacon's obsessive representations of the shameful, tragic decease of his former lover, George Dyer (never mind the hypocrisy of their inescapable narrative element so defeating to the artist's staunchly proclaimed aesthetic of no meaning in a meaningless universe). Bacon consistently denies story-telling as legitimate to his and, indeed, any painter's visual strategies. According to Farson, "[*Triptych, May—June 1973*] can ... be seen as a form of tribute or, more callously, as an exploitation because he was fascinated by the starkness of the subject"[64] That it is his lover's death appears in no way to diminish the fascination.

In one way or another, pretty well all of Bacon's painting comes from the nihilistic dismissal of redemptive qualities and regenerative meaning in life, although the character itself of the artist's

---

[61] "Dying on the Toilet" by Max Porter, *the Paris Review*, June 13, 2016, offers a compelling tribute to the *Triptych* and the personal validation that he experienced in the presence of its uncompromising depiction of event. The discussion here centres on the claim that the mere fact of experience is not sufficient for attribution as a work of art. Were it to be otherwise, the door would be open to endless horror not to mention banality.

[62] Peppiatt, *Francis Bacon: Anatomy of an Enigma*, 71-72.
"Bacon does not dissociate pleasure from pain and can imagine as a matter of plain fact people should literally 'die of love' — be beaten to death, that is to say, in the course of transports that get out of hand." — Russell, Francis Bacon, 129.

[63] p.151.

[64] Farson, *The Gilded Gutter Life of Francis Bacon*, 192.

delivery often, and especially in the later portraits, argues against this. For Taylor, the judgment of the art world, in this case, is wrong. (Other voices in the wilderness concur but appear to be few or restrained.) He provides lengthy "Keys" at the back of each canvas in the indicting triptych for the complete understanding of his intentions.

The Universe of Francis Bacon

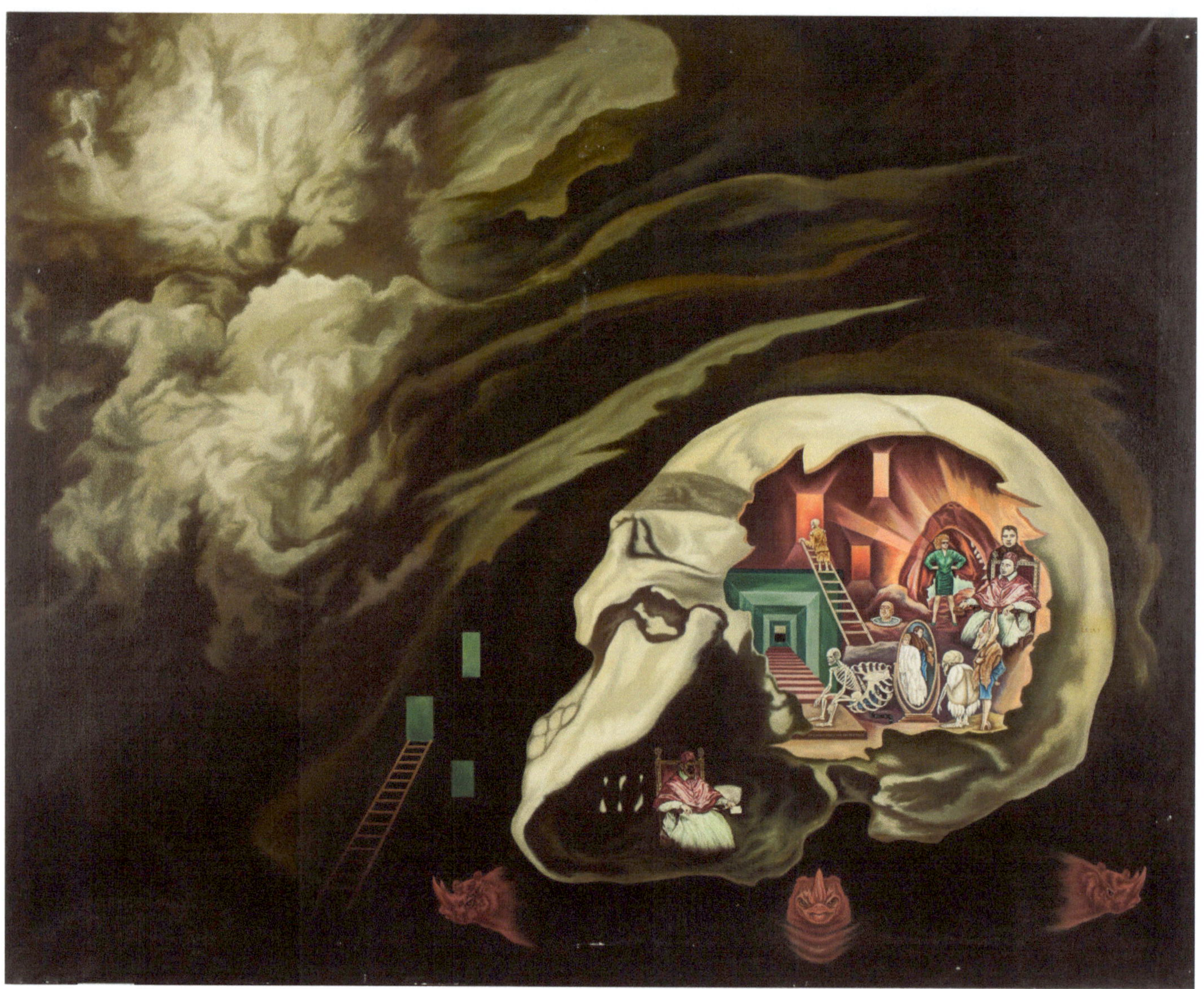

The Universe of Francis Bacon, 1990

In the first panel, if the skull — Bacon's skull — exposed to view as if by a hammer blow, was to think, the group of individuals circumscribed within this particular artifact would represent its thoughts. All the figures are subject to the gaping, leviathan killer-shark maw that attends in the background of the group arrangement. In the "explanatory poem," here referred to as KEY, written on the back of the canvas, Taylor attributes this image to El Greco's *Dream of Philip II,* with the pointed comment that, "its hoard of broken souls,/Did not concern his Catholic Majesty." In Philip's stead, a complacent, possibly resigned Francis

52

Bacon stands as the archetypal arbiter behind the enthroned papal figure that so obsessed and compelled him to produce some forty-five "meaningless" (following Bacon) versions of it.

Here, Taylor's pope fixes a masked gaze upon a modern Salomé, who offers an invitation to all comers while flanked by the shark's fangs, mouth open like a monstrous vagina. Rising to her challenge, the pope's phallus complements his focused look.

The eyeglasses of a peering victim at the archetypal whore's feet might be identifying this beheaded John-the-Baptist-on-a-platter as one of the laudatory art critics — "reduced to a mere John" as the KEY has it — who have anointed the British painter. The figure's eyes are turned upwards to where three windows are cut into the skull, their shafts of red light bathing with damning luminosity a fellow who looks out from the top of a ladder — some blighted visitor seeking escape in a world set alight.

Down from the pope, also at his feet and turned away from him, two society ladies — Bacon's patrons — admire themselves in a full-length mirror unaware that it does not reflect their true bestial nature as it is understood by the recipient of their largesse. From his perspective, the transmogrified skull of one of them also serves for the pope's exposed member.

Behind the looking glass, another, in this instance skeletal, Francis Bacon sits at his toilet that consists of an oversized rib cage. Taylor's KEY makes this identification clear:

> "In loco cordis tui,[65]
> I must ask you to excuse me,
> While I ease myself a little,
> Said the smiling Francis B.

The skeleton's feet are set upon the landing of a stepped corridor leading to a mausoleum-styled enclosure or entranceway whose depths show in the form of light above dark. It is a design of simple construct like two cardboard boxes neatly stored away within a cupboard: the normal, everyday apprehension and arrangement of existence that, for Taylor, is ultimately illusory but that Bacon endorses.

> "Down the false corridor
> Of space and time
> (To harken back to Eliot)
> No footfall sounds.
>
> 'Only the wind
> And nada, nada, nada'"[66] KEY

A more accurate rendition of Bacon's famous, repeated, dismissive treatments of Velasquez's pope occupies the jaw of the skull. A set of six portcullis fangs obtrudes from the darkness at his side. The besmirched Holy Father clutches what would be a form of papal bull — apparently its wasted light causing a window to form in the jaw bone. He is about to drop it at his feet that are shrouded in brown smoke signifying yet one more form of Bacon:

---

[65] "In loco cordis tui ibi defaeco. 'In the place where your heart was, there I defecate' — inscribed beneath the defecating skeleton on the thirteenth stair in the painting, and here suggested as an appropriate motto for the spirit of denial and negation from which so many of Bacon's paintings appear to emanate. The figure itself and its activity are derived from a theme common in Bacon's painting."

[66] One of Bacon's pet phrases.

> "Another figure, dressed in brown,
> Curled like smoke
> Around Velasquez's desecrated pope ..." KEY

The red light that fills the skull has faded into a watery carpet-like desert underfoot — nothing to alarm. All is understood with the head or face of the arbitrating Bacon serving as an enlarged all-seeing eye of the ready-to-devour shark ("no partial occultation/Doubled herewith/In the face of Francis Bacon" KEY). On the front of the canvas, Taylor inscribes,

> "And What Is The View From The Skull
> But A View From The Skull?"

This loaded question contains its own answer and reminds the viewer of the non-meaningful foundation of Bacon's work as first established in his *fons et origo* Crucifixions. Once the painter has subscribed to a life without meaning beyond the response of his own nervous system, he can expect to find exactly that and nothing else.

Three tusked, red-bodied, thick-skinned rhinoceroses — emblematic brutality — swim supportively in the murky waters beneath the skull. Taylor, however, does not leave matters there. He has no one to climb the single ladder to the three ascending windows he places outside the cranium, whose promise of a green prospect suggests a counter vision to the crimson "view from the skull":

> "But I had turned away from things unseen
> The weather showed a nascent smil, [sic]
> Beyond a casement giving on the green
> Spring rains were falling quietly
> All the while." KEY

Bacon's explanation for his preferred treatment of the human mouth as screaming in horror and pain, as Taylor also notes on the canvas back, endlessly references the line that the English painter apparently takes to be the summation of Aeschylus's literary thought — "The reek of human blood smiles out at me."[67] Bacon never failed to embrace this inversion of the human smile, whose convenient cancellation of its significance allowed him to concentrate upon its opposite:

> "The cry itself is fundamentally ambiguous, betokening rage, pain, fear or the pleasure of sexual release with little differentiation. It was this enigmatic combination that fascinated the sadomasochistic artist: in the spasm that made man indistinguishable from beast, human nature could at last be glimpsed as it really was. For Bacon, whose genius dictated the shortest way to the heart of existence, the cry was the indisputable moment of truth."[68]

---

[67] This favourite quotation of his from the *Oresteia* also translates as "the reek of human blood is laughter to my heart." — a more contextual rendering. *The Gilded Gutter Life of Francis Bacon*, 133.

[68] Peppiatt, *Francis Bacon: Anatomy of an Enigma*, 172.

It is perhaps telling that he found the painting with the most famous smile of all "boring." - Archimbauld, *Francis Bacon In Conversation*, 37.

The Universe of Francis Bacon II (The Outward Vision Leads Nowhere)

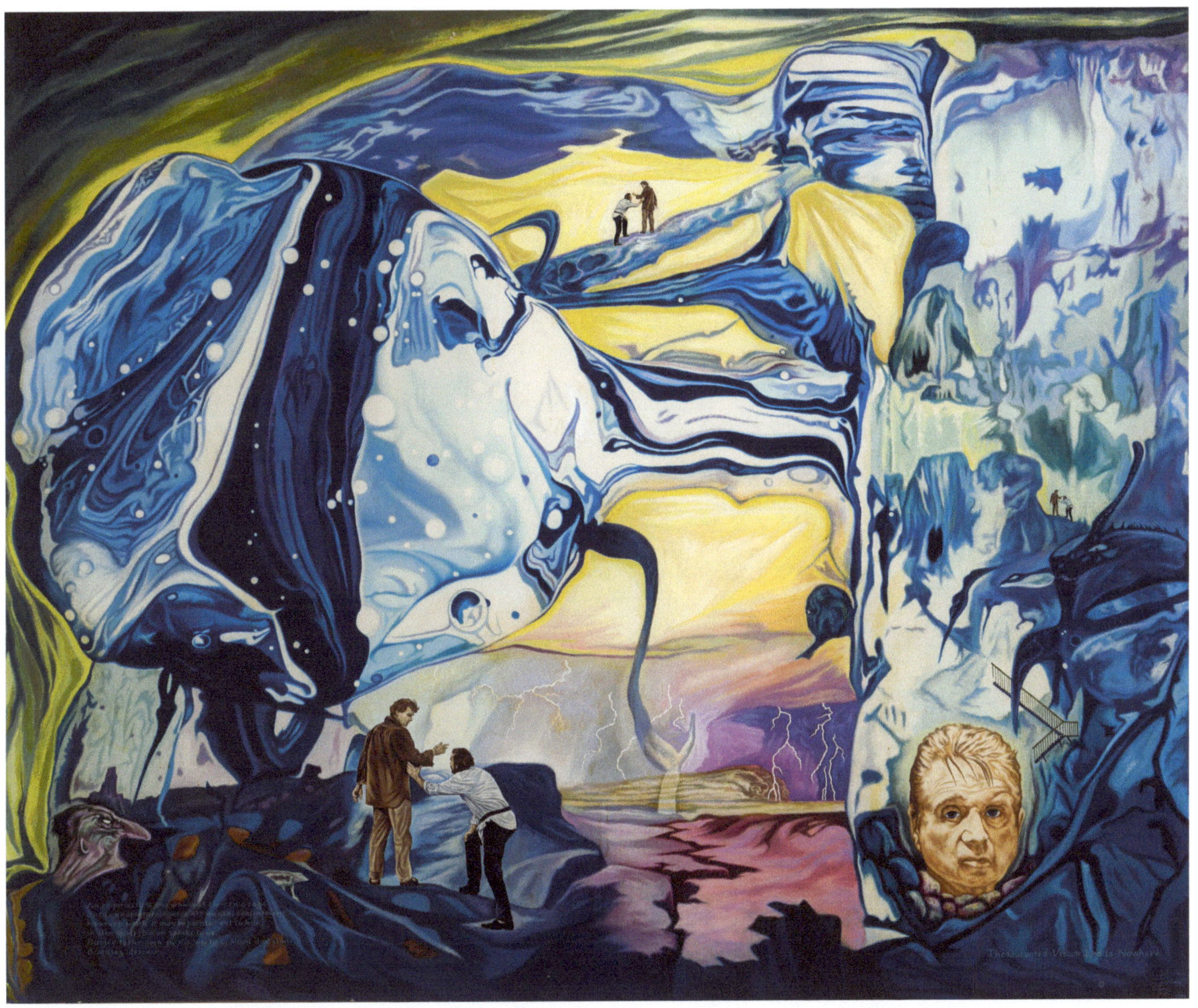

The Universe of Francis Bacon II (The Outward Vision Leads Nowhere), 1991

The central panel of Taylor's Bacon triptych, showing no regard for its subject's detestation of all forms of metaphysics, lays out a symbol-rich deconstruction of the meaning of Bacon's nihilism wherein his "paintings could only reflect some inexplicable fragment of the vast, meaningless whole."[69] The immediate and lasting impression is of a minimally active universe that is entirely biological in nature ("we live, we die and that is all" in Bacon's words). Its jaundiced anaemic palette, awash with cold pervading blues (not the kindest effect upon the eye — Taylor sets aside any allowances here), illustrates the spirit of Bacon's dismissal. Text on the front of the canvas describes its subject as "buried to the neck in his world of blood and stone/Breeding despair."

The head of Bacon directs a gaze of invitation for the viewer to enter his world where staircases lead from nowhere to nowhere. Opposite, at the left foreground, two animalistic figures representing his "un-glossed" self (as he might phrase the self-described brutality of his true nature) have "emerged

---

[69] Peppiatt, *Francis Bacon, Anatomy of an Enigma*, 333.

from [their] Plato's cave," according to KEY at back of canvas, and look with horror and trepidation upon a universe where all to be seen is an image of their own vacuity. From this "pointless" perspective,

> "…the only egress is back to the material world across a … Bridge of Sighs — a vaginal passage through which metaphysical spermatoza [sic] (some confused) inseminate the tripartite world of nature: body, mind (darkened) and soul, from whose skies (and human hopes) the devourer of worlds, Leviathan, with looking-glass eye, sweeps away a third of the stars with his tail. He is the serpent of *Genesis*, the great fish of Jonah, the Great Red Dragon of Revelation, but here portrayed in white [emerging from his caul] — his most forbidding aspect, as Melville holds." KEY

Two travellers — one who has accepted the British painter's invitation, the other warningly attempting to draw his companion away — "wander to no end through Bacon's world." KEY The weed-like rendition of the tree of the knowledge of good and evil, umbilically connected to this cosmic or universal Leviathan, barely survives in the barren, cleaved ground and appears to be fading into nothingness as it feeds "the philosophic premises [on which] he [Leviathan/Bacon] is dependent for his existence and nourishment." KEY

On the front of his canvas, Taylor writes:

> "An empiricist is one who was born in a cage
> But is unable to recognize his mental confinement."

He doubtless has at least partially in mind Bacon's posing of his numerous portrait figures within fixed, sharply delineated boundaries — ironically in this case confines of the nonexistent spirit. The critic Russell considers the implication in structural terms of these spaces carved out within rooms:

> "The cage-like surround which locates each of them so precisely is not, of course, to be taken literally. It is simply a space-bending device; and in conjunction with the mirrors … pulls our attention back to the seated figures."[70]

The inevitably contorted figures also present as having internalized their containment. It is now a part of their identity — a prison within a prison within a prison. Not so much a process of evolution but one of acceptance and submission has occurred from the paintings where, Peppiatt comments, "Bacon returned obsessively to depicting the scream in anonymous figures seated alone in sealed rooms …"[71] Perhaps, to take Bacon at face value in his disclaimers of narrative content, his paintings then should be approached as representing something on the order of "visualizations of cognitive sensation" issuing from subjects solely conscious of their nothingness within a mortal coil. Left unanswered would be the source of the primal objection. Why is his brute matter/nature not content to be itself?

---

[70] Russell, *Francis Bacon*, 138.
[71] Peppiatt, *Francis Bacon: Anatomy of an Enigma*, 171.

Taylor's painting *The Rule of Either/Or (Three Persons Within a Pyramid Shape)* draws upon the dark and imprisoning geometry of the monstrous Egyptian desert artifact, so mesmerizing to tourists and strongly rejected by the visionary eighteenth century poet William Blake as antithetical to the world of the imagination and freedom of the spirit. The use of chains to outline the pyramid form makes clear that the depiction is of a state of mind subject to choice, the figures not imprisoned but rather considering the implications of the construct:

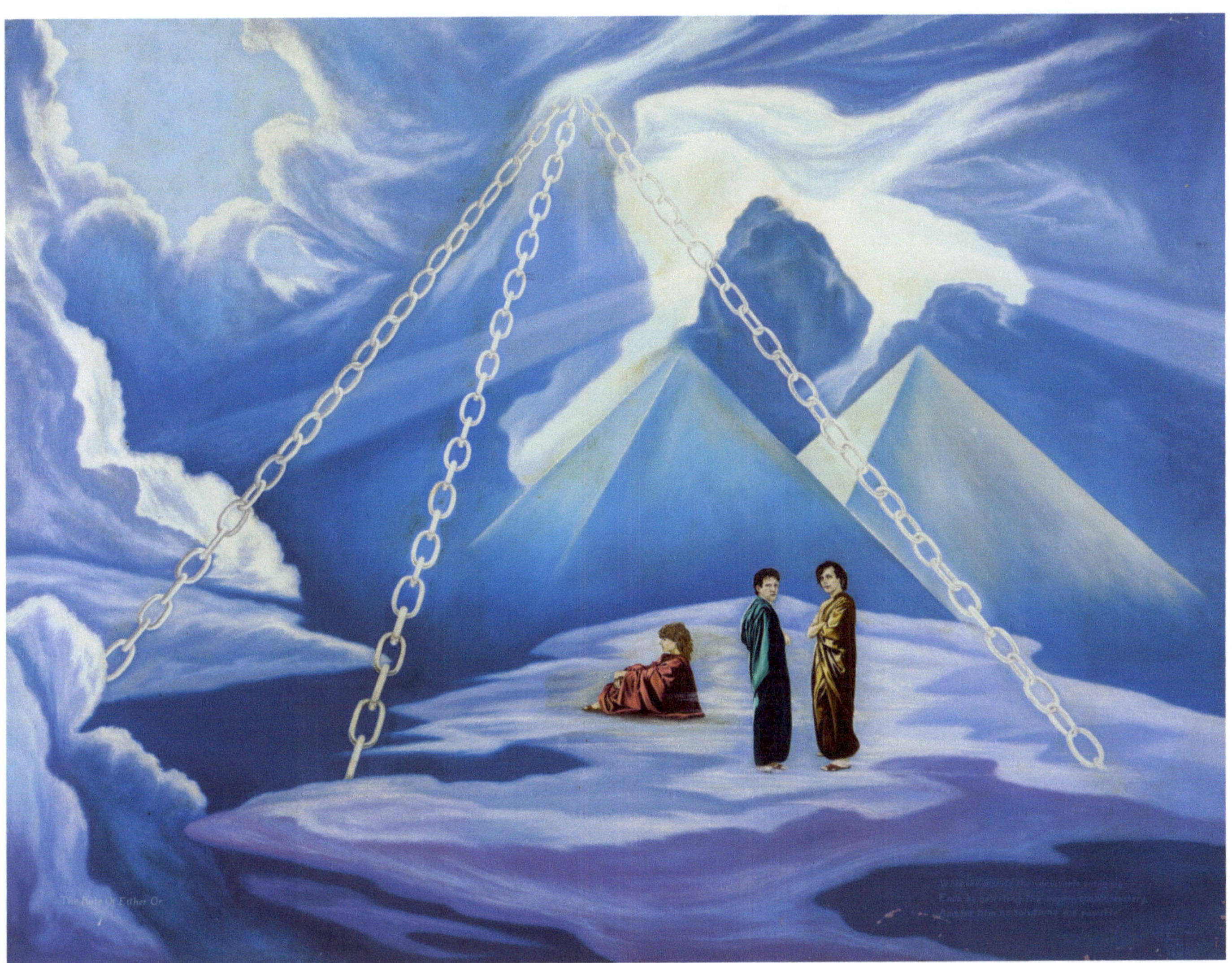

The Rule of Either Or (Three Persons Within A Pyramid Shape), 1987

For Bacon, the art of ancient Egypt represented the summit of aesthetic achievement.[72] If Taylor's paintings intend anything — and they are certainly replete with meaningful intention — it is to identify and, emphatically, to liberate whatever suffers from unnecessary threat and confinement.

---

[72] "[T]he monuments that he visited confirmed his belief that Egyptian art was the highest form of visual expression ever achieved by man." - *Francis Bacon: Anatomy of an Enigma*, <u>ibid.</u>, p.168.

The Apotheosis of Francis Bacon

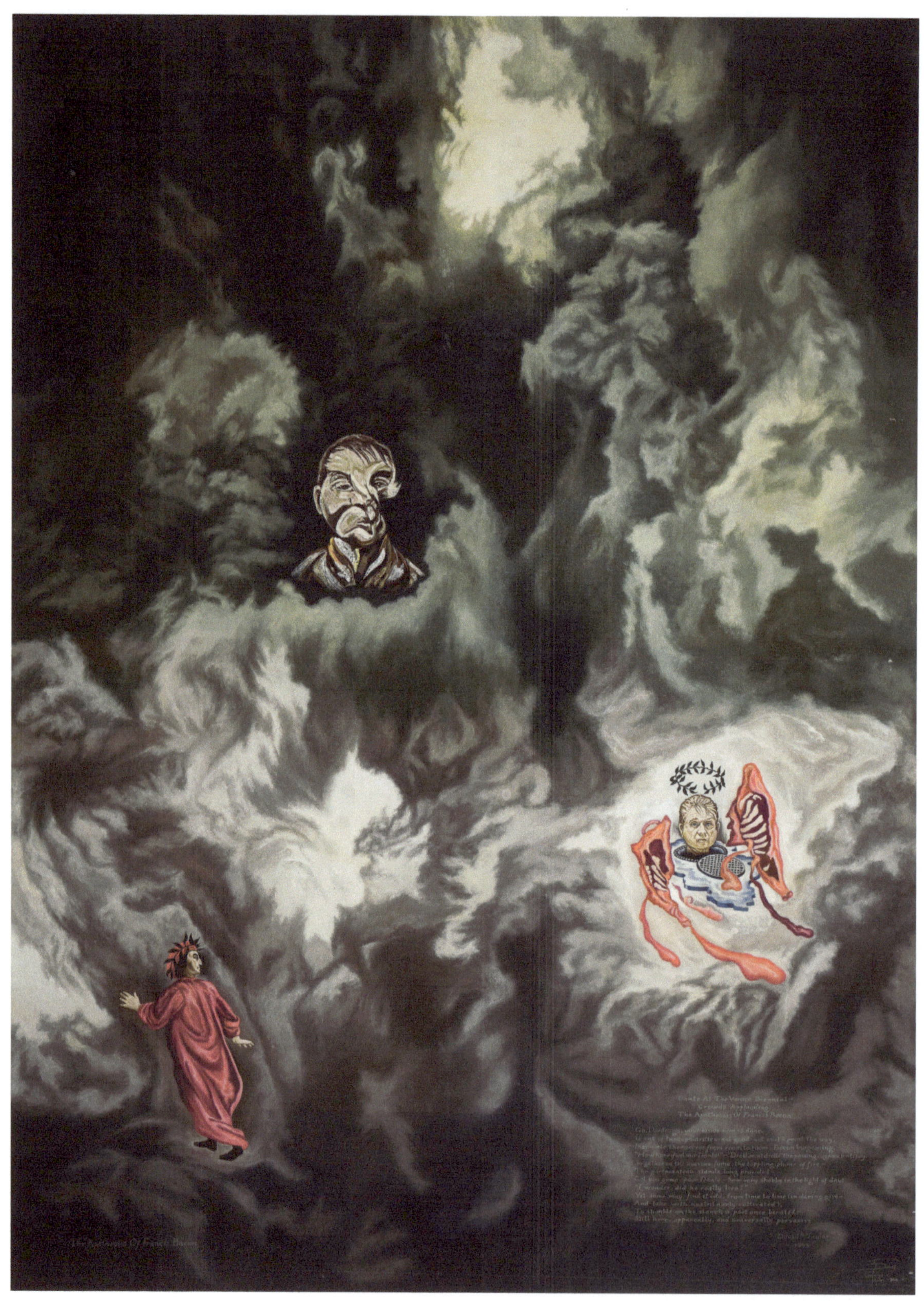

The Apotheosis of Francis Bacon, 1994

Die-hard Bacon enthusiasts cannot help but be scandalized by the triptych's concluding note of disrespect for the art world contemporary with Taylor as it draws from the facts of their idol's life. However, admirers who recall Bacon's social and artistic adventures should find the irony of its depiction amusing, blasphemous though it be to the anointed deity of 20th century painting — its proclaimed "greatest" practitioner. Once again, the focus is on a head, here receiving its secular honours in laurel-haloed form as it emerges from an open manhole flanked by bleeding slabs of meat (as Bacon once famously posed himself for a *Vogue* shoot),[73] whose "beauty" the painter took it upon himself to propound <u>ad nauseum</u> to an aesthetically gullible world and whose essence he ever insisted represents the entire truth of existence ("We are meat ... meat!"). Baleful and unrepentant, this parallel to the John the Baptist image in the first panel of the triptych continues to stare directly and unashamedly, as in the second panel, at the viewer. In his own terms, he can expect no greater ascension considering that, from his *fons et origo* onwards, he identifies life itself as crucified meat.

Frontal text, under the heading "Dante At The Venice Bienniel[sic]/Crowds Applauding/The Apotheosis Of Francis Bacon," warns away the peripatetic figure who authored the *Divine Comedy*:

> "Go, Dante, go: your vision now is done
> Is out of tune; polarities — not good, not evil — point the way,
> Insinuate themselves from room to room: Bacon burgeoning."

(Bacon's placement of figures, "burgeoning" in a seemingly endless series of claustrophobic rooms would be one interpretation.) Dante would be included in Bacon's cavalier dismissal of the merits of vast swathes of artistic achievement. By his own admission, he is immune to the claims of any number of painters, composers and writers — past and contemporary. If they do not reflect his worldview, their work apparently cannot or does not deserve to find a response in his highly specialized sensibility, or as he more biologically terms it, his "nervous system." The same would have to hold true for his similarly sophisticated, cultish devotees.

The Renaissance poet himself shows "very shabby in the light of day," and "'Droll, most droll!' the passing cognoscenti say,"[74] as he looks askance at the dubious emergence of the acclaimed painter from the excremental depths of the 20th century. Dante is, however, well-versed in such matters that Bacon's contemporaries hardly dare to raise:

> "... some may find it odd from time to time (in daring give-
> and-take with nostril nicely cultivated),
> To stumble on the stench a poet once berated —
> Still here, apparently, and universally pervasive."[75]

---

[73] "When [John] Deakin photographed him for *Vogue*, he flanked him with carcasses suspended on hooks. Francis commented: 'Yes, that was rather amusing'." <u>ibid</u>, 134.

The parallel construction to the Crucifixion paintings is clear.

[74] On the front of the canvas.

[75] Front of canvas.

On the 8th Circle of Hell, the poet is "assailed by a terrible stench, for here the FLATTERERS are immersed in excrement." — *Divine Comedy*, Canto XVIII, 134.

The ascendant visage of Bacon as presiding deity, rendered in his familiar painting style of psychological contortion, holds court within a "noxious … toppling plume"[76] — an inversion of the traditional visionary fire of revelation. Fumes gather and rise about the confrontation between the two laurel-crowned icons of art and literature, both subject to this warped, triumphantly judgmental, uncompromising and richly turned out "apotheosis" figuration. Taylor disdains to complete the crowning in the sewer-dwelling Bacon's case

Taking Roger Fry's comments on the essential spiritual significance of all the greatest art further, condemnatory text on the back of the canvas adds to what Taylor has wrought visually on the front:

> "Art that neither emanates from nor addresses a human sense of soul is, at root, fraudulent; its instinct is to consign itself and the world around it — whether sooner or later — to annihilation." [italics are in reference to Bacon's oft-stated reliance solely upon instinct for the direction his painting took]

He precedes this with an indictment of Bacon's treatment of his former lover that accordingly establishes a familial "tradition" going back to his famous forebear:

> "*Tradition*
> "Elizabethan Francis Bacon betrayed his friend Lord Essex
> (He who made his fortune) to the block;
> Gave him the cool and calculated nod.
>
> "Descendant Francis Bacon: much the same for one George Dyer;
> A cool and calculated painting showed him puking, dying naked
> On the john — the world might see; another friend to Bacon — poor
> dim sod."

A textual enlistment of Tolstoy further castigates Bacon's admirers:

> "'It never enters anyone's head that to admit a greatness not commensurable with … [a] standard of right and wrong is merely to admit one's own nothingness and immeasurable littleness.'"[77]

Over time, the insights and accomplishments of the world's great artists have engendered a cultural consensus whereby all that lies within the scope of the inquiring human mind, not merely one view or another, appropriately deserves consideration as presenting or approaching aspects of truth in nature and in reality. This is not to say that the nihilistic conclusion in response to the various traumas of the human condition ought not to have its place in an either/or surmise; however, if life does in fact have inherent meaning of a broadly encompassing embrace, it may very well in the end be impossible for the attentive artist to resist.

Michael Peppiatt, one of Bacon's many sympathetic critics, appears to be moving in this direction when he responds to the painter's later work:

---

[76] Front.
[77] *War and Peace,* Bk IV, Part III, Ch.18.

"There are flashes in a painting like the Three Studies for a Portrait of John Edwards (1984) of the supernatural atmosphere that makes Shakespeare's last plays so magical. Here, the figures are so much less distorted as to become almost naturalistic; *they appear to rise for the first time* above their inherent confusion as self-consciously mortal creatures."[78] [italics mine]

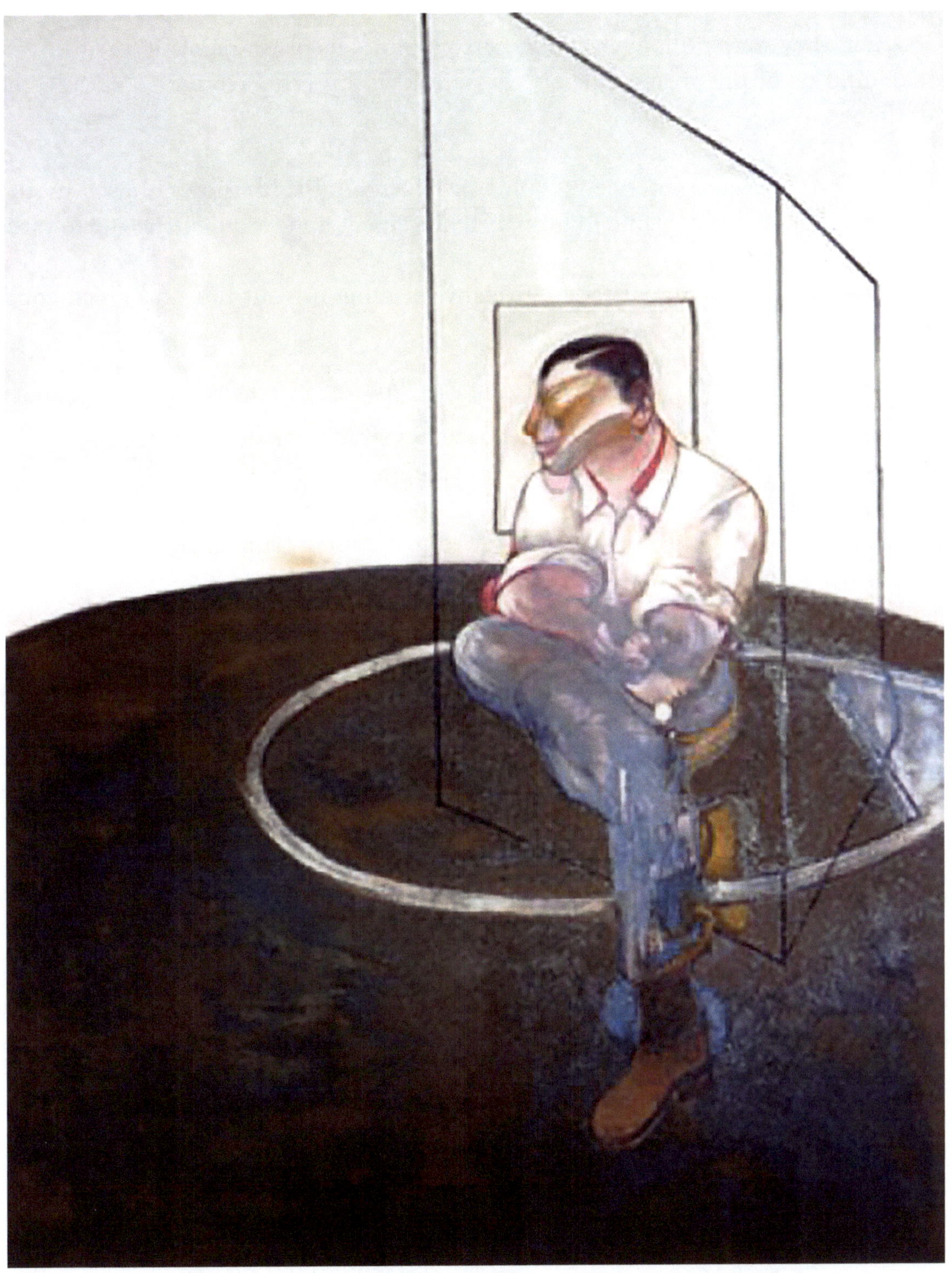

Right Panel of *Three-Studies-for-Portrait-of-John-Edwards*, 1984

---

[78] Peppiatt, *Francis Bacon: Anatomy of an Enigma*, 355.

In a similar vein, John Russell recalls,

> "[T]he painter Frank Auerbach ... said that Bacon's portraits were 'like risen spirits'. Where the subjects were still living, the portraits were, in effect, like effigies that he held high in the face of their certain and possibly imminent dissolution.

> "When they were no longer living, he sometimes went on painting them in ways that remind us of the great challenge thrown down by John Donne ... 'Death, thou shalt die'."[79]

Bacon, in his later reflective interviews with Michel Archimbauld, shows himself more willing to entertain notions of an enduring value to human achievement and internalizing the rewards:

> "As it is, it's so rare to manage to give any meaning to your life, and it's so good if you do succeed."[80]

According to Helen Lessore in *Partial Testament*, "[T]he truth is that Bacon's works are great religious paintings. ...The very agony of his unbelief becomes so acute that, by the intensity of its involvement with final questions, the negative becomes as religious as the positive".[81] For his part,

> "Bacon insisted that his painting be viewed in a kind of biographical vacuum ... [although] 'My whole life goes into my painting.'"[82]

It may very well be that Taylor, unlike Bacon, was fortunate in his personal circumstances having enjoyed a childhood without abuse and, in addition, having begun his painting career some time after the first half of the twentieth century whose immediate and, in many ways, unique horrors might well result in the blinding of the inner vision.[83] However, his life was not without its own torments, he lived through the same times as Bacon and he was never far from feeling "man's inhumanity to man." His artistic response beginning with *The Sounding of the Seventh Angel* as an affirmation of creative being couldn't be more opposite to Bacon's *Painting 1946* and is a reminder of so many others of like spirit. More recently, shortly after the twin towers fell in New York City, the symphony orchestra from Montreal that was scheduled to put on a concert inquired if it should still come for the event. "Please do!" was the reply. The immediately obvious was not the final story. Something more was needed.

***

---

[79] Russell, *Francis Bacon*, 152.

[80] Archimbauld, *Francis Bacon In Conversation*, 106.

[81] As quoted in Farson, *The Gilded Gutter Life of Francis Bacon*, also of this view, 139.

[82] *Francis Bacon: Anatomy of an Enigma*, 116.

[83] Bacon came to the artist's task with pure talent but, arguably, without the resources to declare let alone affirm meaning and value. The biographies of his early life describe the spiritually eviscerating traumas that he underwent.

Bereft the world of music, painting and literature would be had the Bacon view prevailed before his time or been the sole reference for the human spirit afterwards. Landscape and narrative had no interest for him; however, the art of the Western world is nothing if not redemptive.

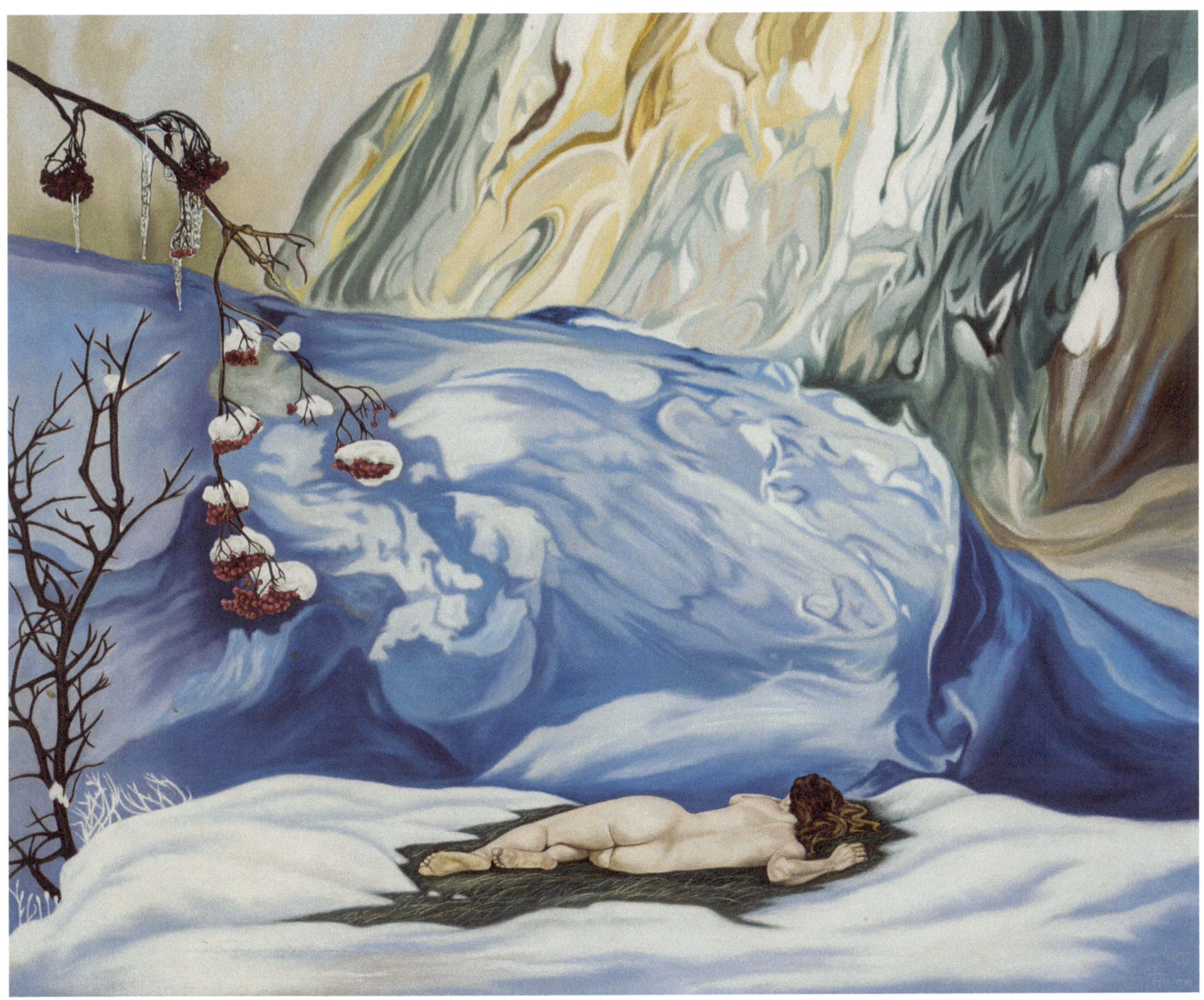

Northern Primavera, 1990

It is easy to feel the affront to Taylor's visual narrative, and how the art world's mute swallowing of the Bacon tenets insults his transcendent concept of the aesthetic personality. He defends it against those whose views put it at existential threat.

The artist declares a substantial and transformative identity to states of being. *Northern Primavera* places an archetype firmly and comfortably in the bosom of the "great white north" with a young lady lying odalisque-like, her back to the viewer in a wintry landscape, harbinger and personification of the spring that will come and that, at the same time, emanates from her as it does from all about her. When she awakens, the world will be transformed. Her mere presence in its correspondence with the landscape brings about an alchemical shift that will be returned. Vision formed by and fused with selected materials is the vehicle of the artist's discourse; once again to Taylor's distinction between the artist's social and aesthetic personality in *The Aesthetic Theories of Roger Fry Reconsidered:*

"Of a decidedly contrary mind, I. A. Richards asserted, 'When we look at a picture, or read a poem, or listen to music, we are not doing something quite unlike what we were doing on our way to the Gallery or when we dressed in the morning.' As Fry's answer to this position, in his … analysis of Rembrandt's 'A Schoolboy at his Desk' so clearly reveals, the main value afforded us by the true (or hypothetically 'pure') work of art is the experience of the uniquely transmutational force of the individual artist's sensibility as it operates upon experience."[84]

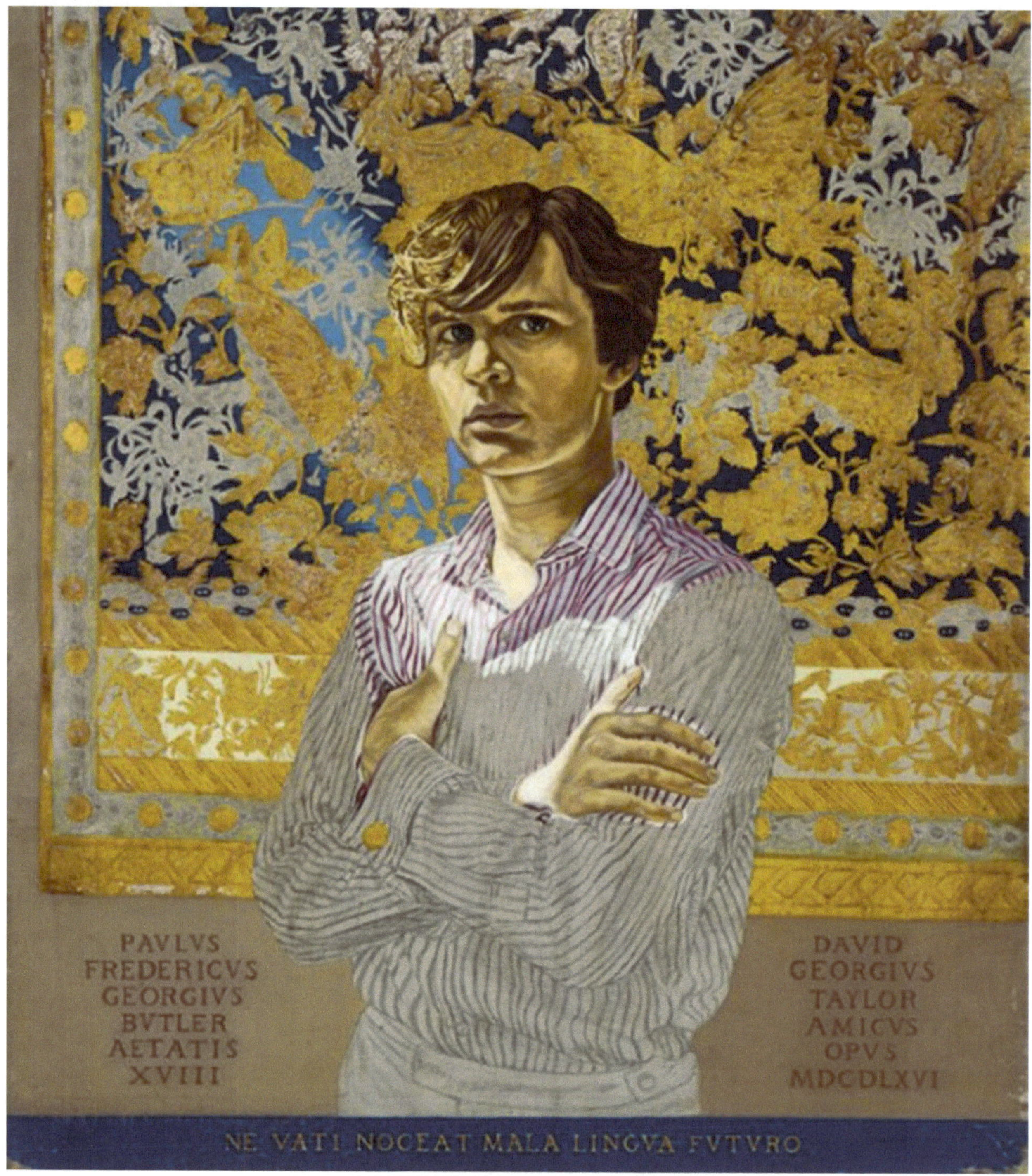

Portrait of Paul Butler, c. 1968

---

[84] <u>Op.cit.</u>, 63.

"Do not cast aspersions on the future poet," translates the Latin text at bottom of Taylor's early unfinished portrait of his student friend, which he paints at a time when he is completely oblivious to what Bacon is up to. The sole similarity that might be found between the two painters would be the modern feel of their styling. What emanates from Taylor's canvas is neither tortured, confined nor conflicted. Rather, it is backed by the detailed, timeless beauty of what the human spirit can work.

A later commissioned portrait betrays no loss of faith or insight. The effect of time has been to confirm and to mature:

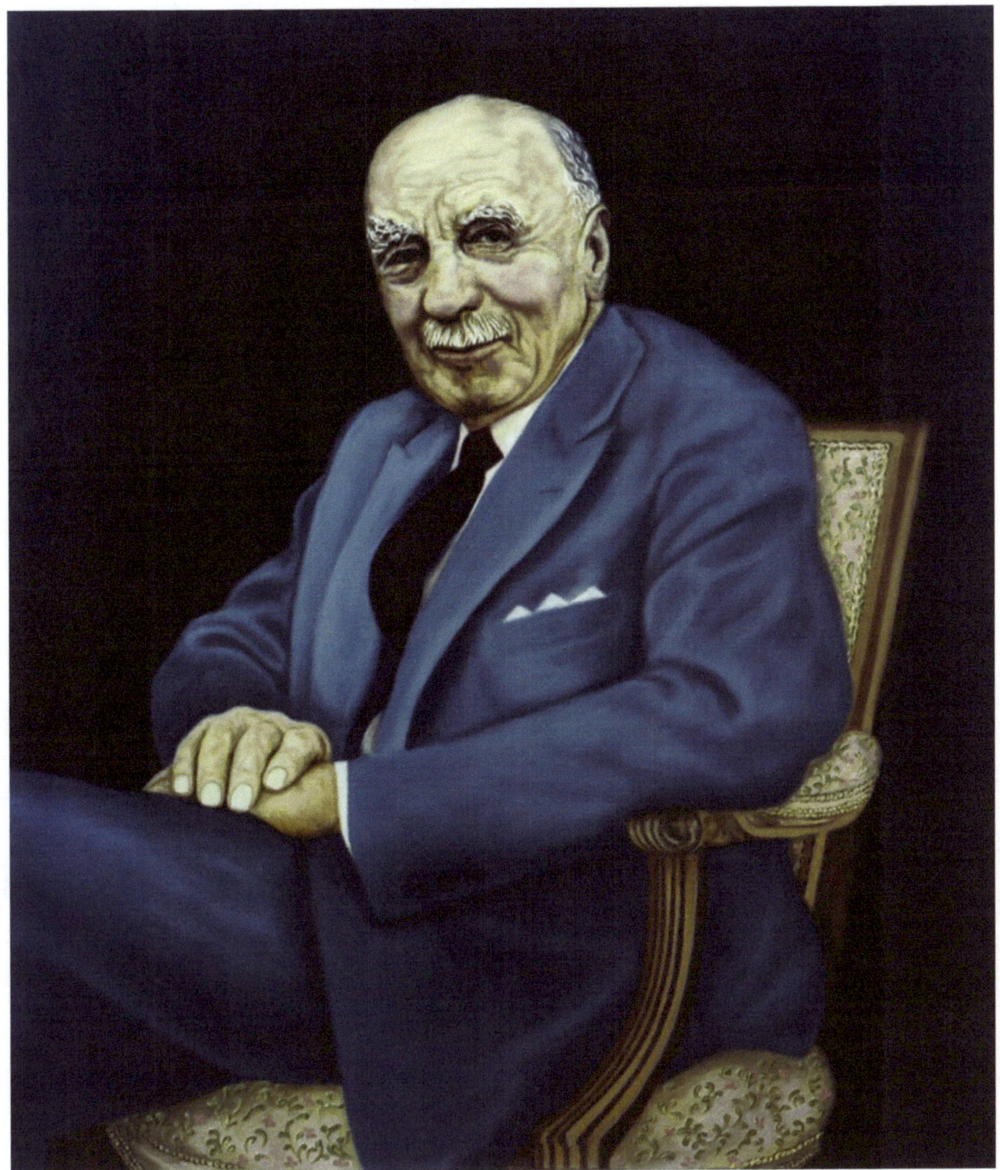

Portrait Of Paul Aubin de la Messuzière, c. 1980

Taylor quotes Roger Fry on Rembrandt and the Master's handling of his materials:

"'…it reveals so intimately the mysterious play of light upon matter that it becomes *the vehicle of a strangely exalted spiritual state, the medium through which we share Rembrandt's deep contemplative mood.*'"[85]

---

[85] Roger Fry, *Transformations,* op.cit.

CHAPTER IV

The Visionary Landscape

Throughout his career, Taylor posits a deeper reality to self and to the world at large than everyday human social communication of these matters, at least on its surface, would suggest. In his visionary symbolic period, he explores, discovers, expands upon the nature of the human, in this case aesthetic spirit engaged in its creative tasks; what are its aims, its expectations, and rewards; what is the source of its energies. He accomplishes this by producing structures of visualized energy, declarations of the artist's informed being inseparable from the created work as it depicts the comprehended world. Having established what is essentially a transcendent identity for the artist and for the artist's subject matter that is fully able to bear witness to all states of being and modes of expression in an infinitely variable, constantly transcending universe, he looks to critique in his visionary figurative period the social preoccupations and attitudes that ultimately deny the possibility, never mind the substantiality of these states.

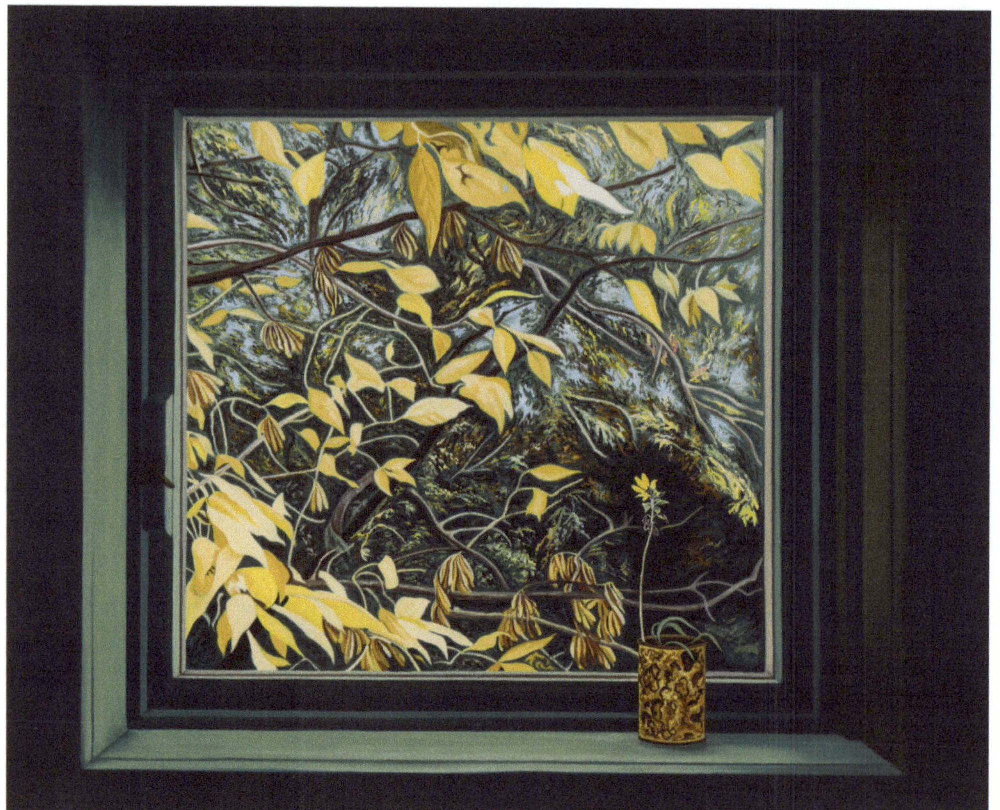

Sunflower In Autumn, 1991

One painting — an occasional piece intended as a gift[86] — attributes, as much as any other Taylor, sentient capacities to the natural world and, further, that are not necessarily foreign or dissimilar to the human. Somewhere he comes upon a sunflower seed that has taken root in a hazardous spot. He transplants it in a can of earth and places this in a studio window with no other intention than to give it the best chance possible — an ordinary event. As the little seedling develops and flowers, he captures on canvas what he sees as its sentient communing with a world of its kind — who hasn't felt the same when strolling through a garden, hiking through a forest, or merely attending to the house plants?

In his visionary landscape period, he inquires into and expresses a heightened and an aesthetic sentience for the natural world, its communing spirit and air of transcendence inescapable to the sensitive observer.

Unlike his placing the oblivious everyday human in the context of a transcendent world (the visionary figurative), he shows the sentience of the natural world as fully participating in and at one with the greater whole. There is no disjuncture between the transcendent assertions of the earlier *Silence* and *Sea Lilies* canvases of the visionary symbolic period and the perceptions that he records in this final period of the visionary landscapes.

The Visionary Landscape

"This nexus of creative emotion is discrete and meditative since so much of its inspiration depends upon a contemplative approach to the natural world: the world as apprehended in terms of a specific medium."[87]

Taylor rarely misses an annual excursion into the wilderness. He can be the most irritating of companions upon these occasions. The practical preparations seem quite beyond him: sufficient and appropriate foods, gear gathered together and in good working order. Not that he doesn't make the effort, but to rely upon him means chaos if not disaster. Items are not arranged in the backpack with thought but thrown in higgledy-piggledy, food, clothing, equipment in intimate congress. He fits nicely into that category of artist who requires a personal attendant to safely navigate life's exigencies. On his first canoe trip in Algonquin Park, he and his friend set out at Lake Opeongo; it seems to be an entire freshwater sea unto itself, the distant shore dipping into obscure unattainability. From the evidence, neither of them has been in such a nervous, skittish craft before this, experiencing its delightful self-harmonizing with an unpredictable world.

They barely survive the crossing, white caps approaching productive of mutual admonitions carried on the wind. At one point, Taylor exclaims, "Do be careful! Don't you realize who is in this canoe with you?" Suffice it to say that the words both outrage and amuse his companion. (Not the desired attitude for the desired outcome.) The winds seem to accompany them the entire trip for the express purpose of their capsize and the sweeping away of their laments and recriminations. After some two weeks, however, at the end of the final leg back to their starting point, the weather in true cliché fashion casts a redemptive, memorializing rainbow before them.

Were he completely incompetent, like a P.G. Wodehouse (who perhaps never would have thought to venture into such a "great outdoors," not knowing how to access his own address), then he might

---

[86] He produced a number of smaller canvases for this purpose over the years.
[87] *The Aesthetic Theories of Roger Fry Reconsidered*, 69.

merit a more perfect compassion, but partial competence tends rather to garner exasperation, impatience and repeated fallings out. Everything is a trial until such time as it receives his approval. The stressed exiting and entering the tent, the turning away from large tree trunks, the balking at having to canoe beneath bridges, add to the disturbed atmosphere. On one trip, his companion writes in his journal: "I am a cloud, floating above all this." The cloud inevitably becomes a boulder and falls to earth. Upon both of them. And yet paintings come from it all.

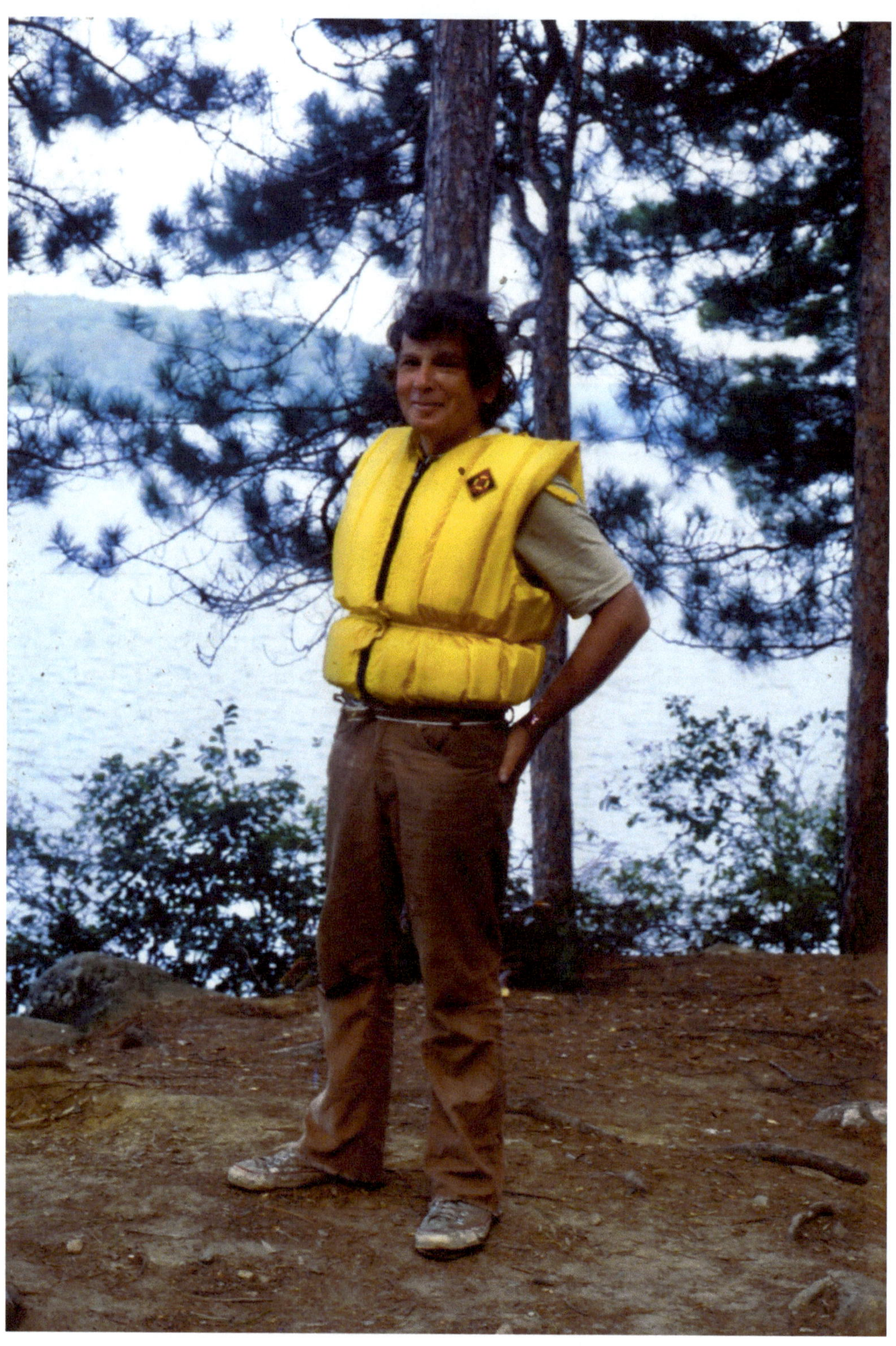

The artist in a yellow life preserver

In Blakean fashion, Taylor early drew upon the biblical narrative to explore and establish his felt understanding of the nature of aesthetic personality and, like the eighteenth century visionary artist, added poetic text to complement and further the visual statement. Having fully established for himself substantial sense of the creative identity, he turned more and more to the world about him, no longer reminting biblical currency, drawing upon other voices and adding his own:

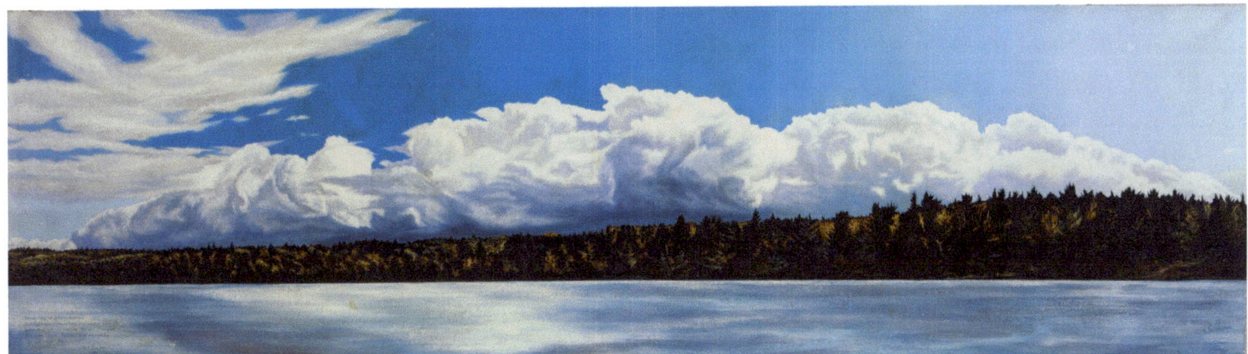

Animoosh, 1986

On the front of the canvas:

"That mass of flesh that circumscribes me,
Limits not my mind. That surface that
Tells the heavens it hath an end,
Cannot persuade me I have any."[88]

Th. Browne, 1635

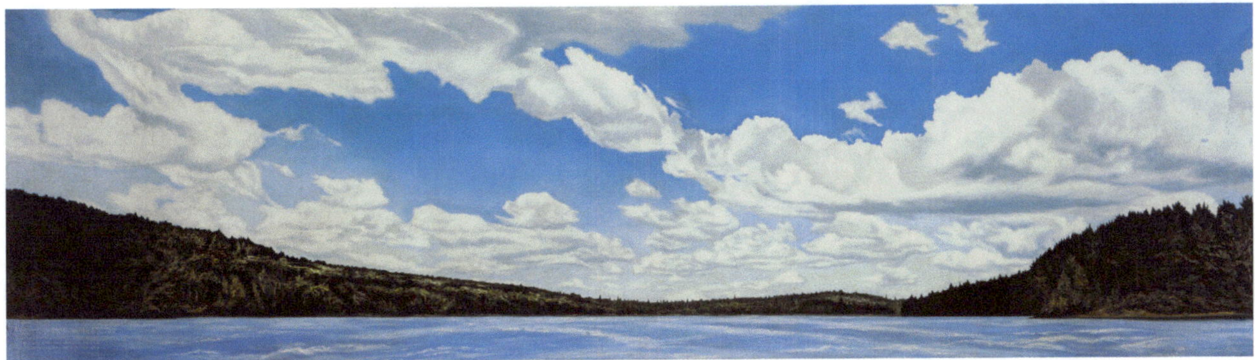

Clamshell Lake, 1988

On the front of the canvas:

Unravelling of golden sleeves,
Sunlight of a momentary, unexpected warmth;
Lowering eyelids and the distant trumpet
Scarcely heard; October and mortality:
Do not linger here.

---

[88] *Religio Medici*, 341.

In the subject matter of *Animoosh* and *Clamshell Lake*, companion paintings of equal dimension, Taylor discerns an inherent spirit whose breadth is not contained either in the limits of human flesh or by the surface of things. He conjoins time and death — "October and mortality" — into a single event without ultimate permanence, the autumnal season itself having no final hold.

The elegance of *Animoosh* renders the painter's spirit as immanent and wedded to its like in the natural world. Some invisible shaping hand manifests in the changing weather and skies burnishing the scene at the pivotal point of darkening light.

Again, *Clamshell Lake* subtly evidences the symbolic, revelatory intentions of the artist's brushwork. As in its companion piece, the lake's water is like a membrane, or the skin of a body that is a vehicle as well as a thing in itself, expressive capacities transcendent; the forest a textual border line, even a barrier of sorts to the unexplored, very present unknown. Like the mirroring waters, the wooded far-flung shore is an image of what the observer sees not the reality of what is there. Disporting, spreading clouds suggest an alternative, a spiritual and liberating universe. The whole of it makes for a singular world reflective of its indispensable parts.

The artist makes a point of stating[89] after completion of his *Equinox* landscape that if there is any meaning to his life's work, it is to be found in this painting. In the face of what went before — the powerful early symbolic canvases, the mid-career philosophic and social commentaries — the natural tendency is to dismiss this apparent devaluation of earlier efforts. More appropriately, his words perhaps should instead be taken as an expression of having arrived at a state of vision that provides ultimate justification to his colloquy with chosen medium. Before concluding that there is little profit left in nature for the attentive artist, one might reflect on what this da Vinci biographer suggests led his subject "into the heart of things:"

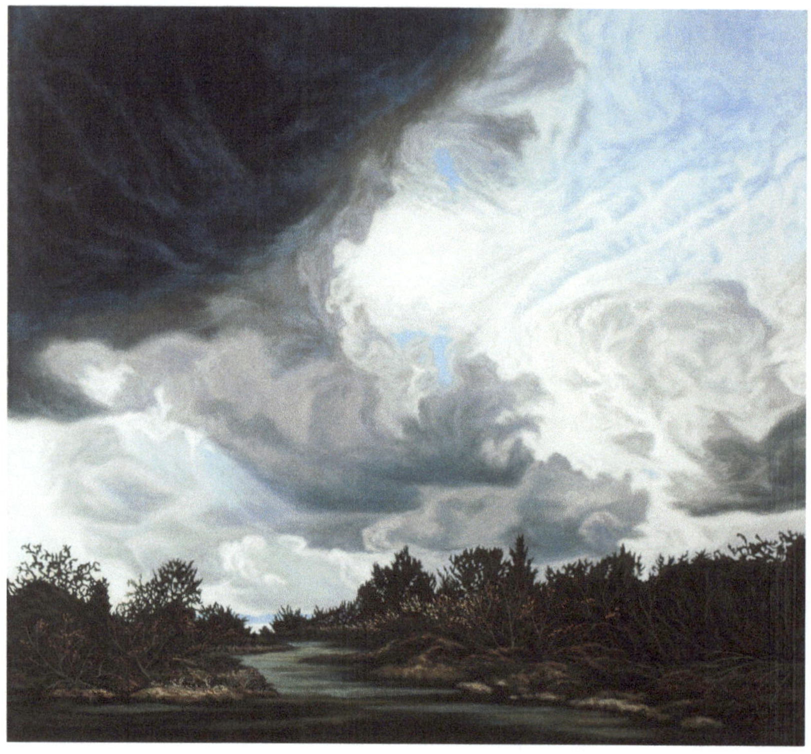

Equinox, 1992

"For Leonardo the key organ in understanding the world is not the brain but the eye. 'The eye, which is called the window of the soul, is the chief means whereby the understanding may most fully and abundantly appreciate the infinite works of Nature,' he [Da Vinci] writes in one of his many *paragoni*, or comparisons, designed to show the superiority of painting over those supposedly more gentlemanly arts like poetry."[90]

Perhaps artists shortchange themselves if they let flag these visual meditations. Recall as well the painter in Virginia Woolf's *To The Lighthouse*, whose canvas calls for repeated efforts on her part before it answers to the queries and demands of her inner vision as it draws upon and does justice to the claims of its subject, their expression an inescapable revelatory aesthetic for the fulfillment of both artist and audience.

---

[89] To his friend.
[90] Charles Nicholl, *Leonardo da Vinci: Flights of the Mind*, (Viking Penguin, 2004), pp.55-56.

A thin snowfall charms an autumn day that it shares with brief lashings of rain and benedictions of sun. The visuals of this elemental dance and its accompanying suggestion of personality make for a painter's ontology and a philosophic genre of landscape. The three elements of sky, forest and horizon, and water are at once separate and yet inextricably connected.

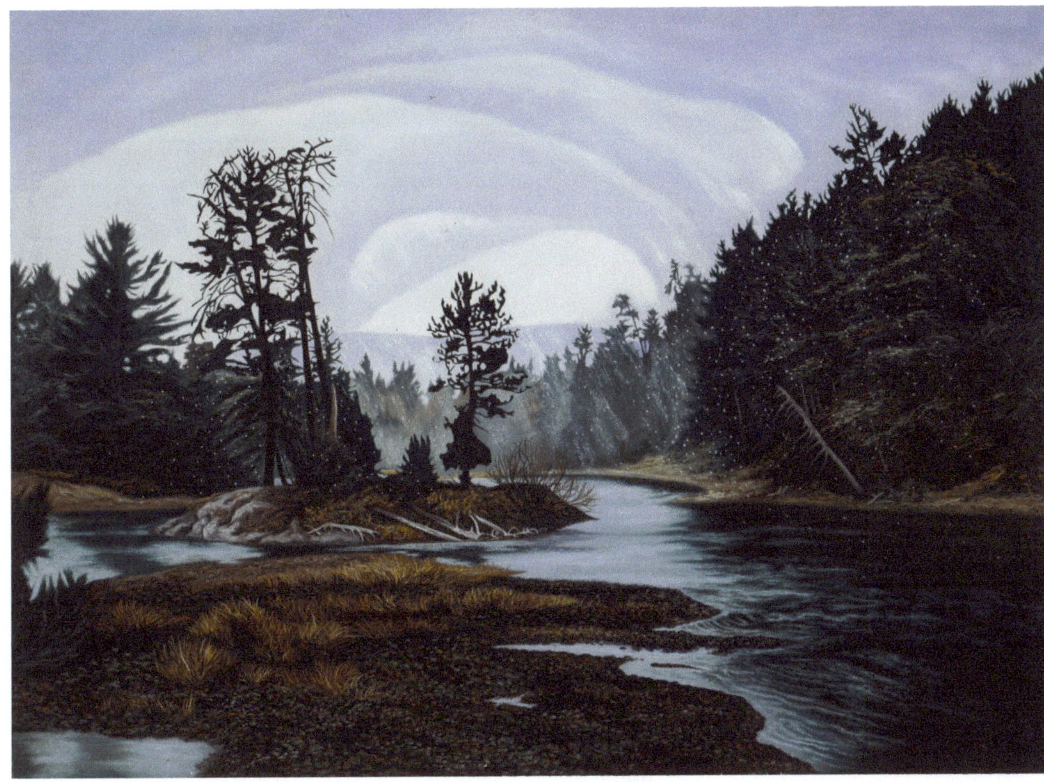

Petawawa River, Late Fall,
1992

"By what magic of handling, by what elusive accents in the tone . . . [Rubens] has managed to colour this literal note of a thing seen, with the special quality of his lyrical feeling." Roger Fry, *French, Flemish and British Art.*[91]

Lady Evelyn Smooth Water River, 1992

Fry's words might equally apply to *Lady Evelyn Smooth Water River.* Only, the artist's written thoughts at the front of the canvas express an aspect of the scene that is independent of him and that moves him to record it.

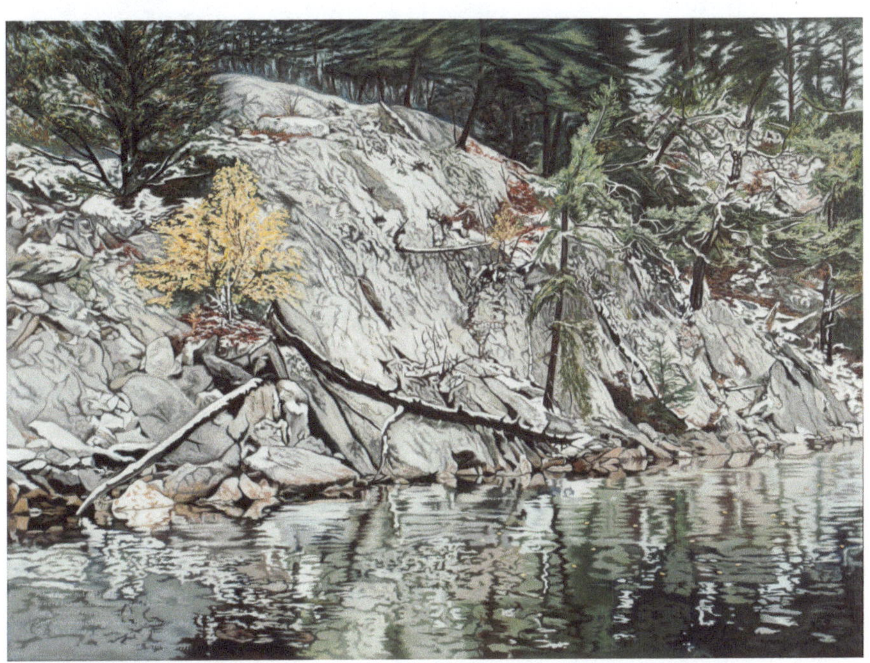

[91] As quoted in *The Aesthetic Theories of Roger Fry Reconsidered,* 71.

> "Ah let me not intrude
> Where russet catchments of old leaves
> Lie Garnered from the wind,
> And amber rustlings, above the mirrored sky,
> Question the dying season's solitude."

It is late fall, when the surface of the river acts upon its propensity to freeze into sheets of thin ice about the canoe. The painting comes from the artist's final excursion into the Canadian wilderness. Failing strength prevents the exertion required to make any more such trips. The aesthetic presence that the work celebrates in the natural world reconciles the painter's spirit to the closing in of winter and sustains it.

***

Valuing all forms of life (with the exception perhaps of piranha — a point of reference in his musings on good and evil), Taylor indulges in a boundless antipathy toward those whose vision he regards as violating and corrupting the world. He has no time for Pierre Elliott Trudeau (and the rest of "that Liberal gang" whom he portrays in the guise of high-placed hit-persons) — seal hunt, seal hunt, seal hunt, wild horses in Alberta rounded up for their meat. The army blockades the Montreal street where he lives and has his studio during the October Crisis. ("How far will I go? Watch me!", proclaims the newly installed leader.) The artist lashes out at the Canadian government, outraged and incensed, as he describes himself to his intimates and in letters to the authorities over the yearly seal hunt and the permission given for the slaughter of the wild horses in the west of the country. *Rogues' Gallery* satirically characterizes the elected members and appointed functionaries as privileged, self-regarding, indifferent and vicious.

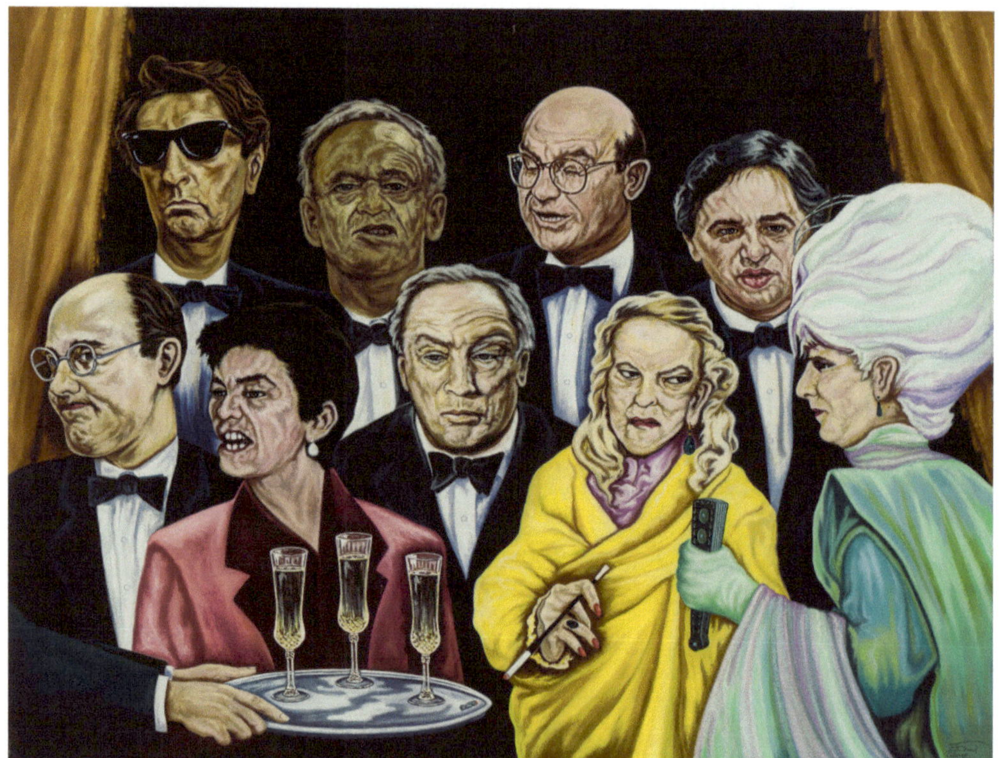

Rogues' Gallery, 1996

Despite his own more personal issues of claustrophobia, agoraphobia and an unrelenting case of pernicious image-retention, he would, however, have to agree with the prime minister, if not in the same insouciant fashion, that the universe has unfolded, in terms of his aesthetic narrative, as it should.[92] Not to say that the conditions for its fulfillment had not needed some extreme nudging on his part, not excluding disruptions to the lives of those about him. He applied himself to the wheel of his chosen destiny at an early age in order to ensure that it headed in the direction best suited to his as yet inchoate, nonetheless partially revealed vision.

His career begins ambitiously with work that visually apprehends and personalizes man's creative energies; from there the focus turns to human society and the mental constraints and attitudes that prevent access to and proper use of this creative identity; he rediscovers what he has always known: these visionary, aesthetic energies and their formative work informing the world of nature. He never fails in his work and in his engagement with those about him to remind and extensively condemn what within mankind poses a threat to them.

He remains fully committed to the subject and significance of aesthetic personality and identity in his painting, a preoccupation perhaps unique among artists to put in visual terms the nature of the artist's being.

> "If the concept of the artist as aesthetic identity or aesthetic personality does involve a categorical substantive distinct from that of the man, in the category of his social identity, then the concepts of self and self-expression as they apply to artistic activity, along with the closely associated concept of artistic process, would seem to have implications far different from those generally associated with the terms."[93]

The requirements of the task he sets himself, calling for painting after painting for its full exposition, cause Taylor to contend that the whole of the work would suffer following the dissemination of its parts and that the significance of the parts themselves would lessen.

> "Taken from the . . . view of process as applied principle of aesthetic selectivity, the entire canon of the artist's work becomes the objectified, – hence available – permanent body of his aesthetic personality, the completed sphere (if he is fortunate) of his emotional, mediumistic cognitions. The central philosophic error of supposing the individual work of art an autotelic identity would seem to involve the failure to recognize the simple enough truth that identity need not preclude variety, and conversely that variety may be an essential feature of an underlying identity."[94]

Ultimately, he is speaking to more than simply his fellow artists. ("One is perfectly aware in looking at one's baby pictures of a thread of identity linking one with that odd little creature . . ." [*Aesthetic Personality*]) Through personality we express our decisions that fundamentally and imaginatively alter out view of ourselves and of life, create our environment, the world that we construct and inhabit; decisions that feed back to personality, to ourselves. We project this personality upon the canvas of life as we pierce through the everyday appearance and circumscription of things, fashioning raw material

---

[92] One of Trudeau's favourite quotes from the prose-poem *Desiderata*.
[93] "Aesthetic Personality", 7.
[94] <u>Ibid</u>, 9.

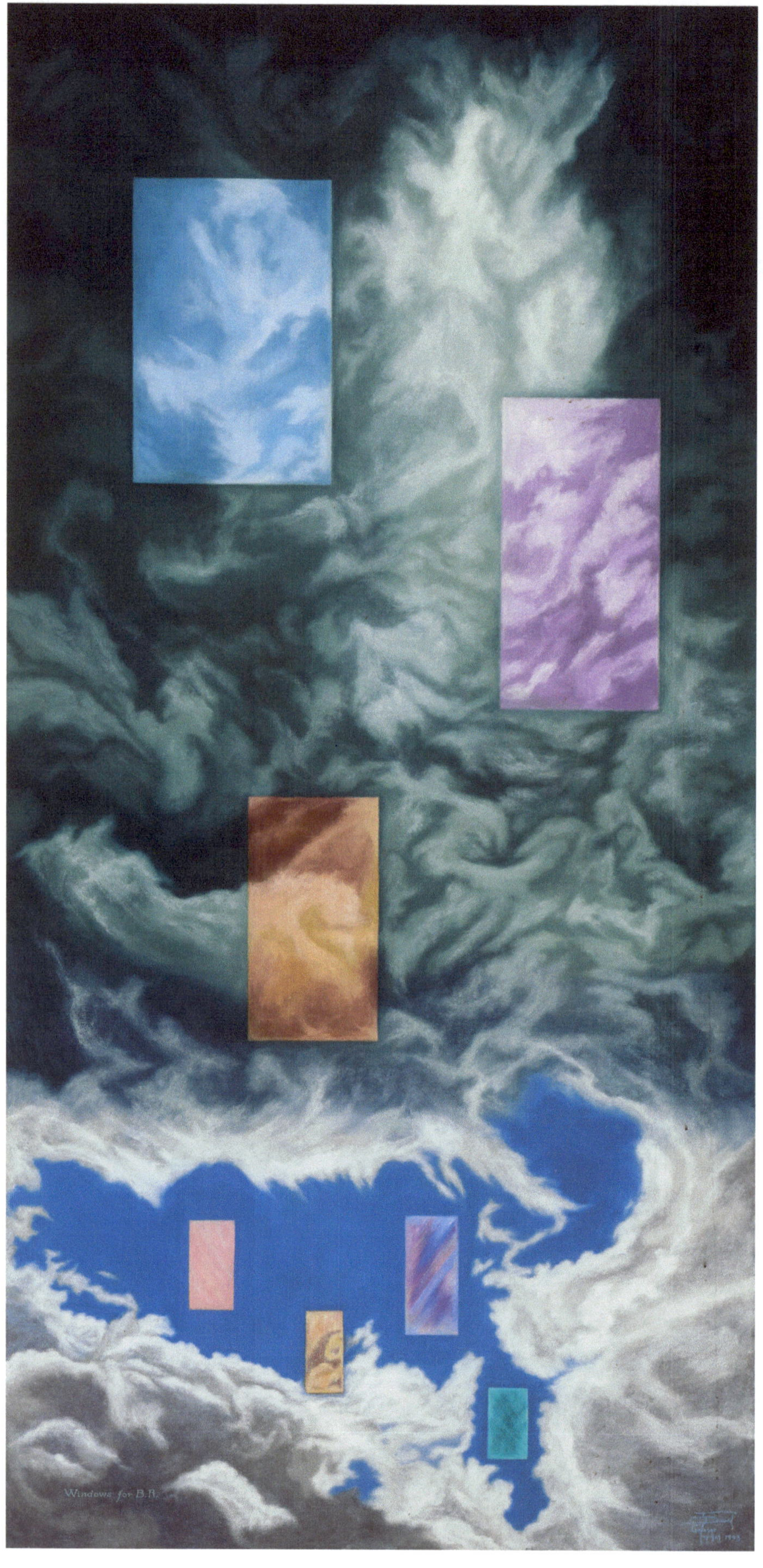

to the needs of our transformative vision. As the poet has written, "Know thyself, and to thine own self be true." Only, how limitless, portentous and generative is the nature of this self that we are urged to know? The poet gives no bounds.

It is ever a work of genius to extend man's understanding of himself; a service, once performed, deserving of acknowledgment and preservation. Like the artist who discovers and realizes aesthetic personality through the colloquy with his art, the being engaged with life similarly discovers and fashions himself/herself through each and every act chosen, thought formulated and entertained, perception gained, emotion nurtured. Is there not some necessarily subsequent and contingent, even altering connection to what we term reality also operative here?

A late painting points to the dangers and pitfalls of self-centred accommodations that constrain and distance the universe:

< *Windows for B.R.*, 1993

A figure such as Bertrand Russell presents yet another bugbear to Taylor, an irresistible adversary impossible not to take on and take down.

On the back of the canvas:

I leaned upon a window sill
Set in a sky of here and now
With somewhere the slow ticking
Of a clock; for time and place
Were here and only here:
A rift between the clouds,
A handful, at the best, of fading stars.
A king frog in his marsh croaked
That he knew the limits of the world,
For he had been around; a thousand
Voices croaked in approbation.
Revered and worldly Bertrand Russell twiddled
With his wireless knob across the dial
(The AM band was all he was equipped
To hear – let's call his philosophic posture AM)
And thus declared the FM others
Talked about was purely sham,
Because there was no evidence
Suggesting, let alone supporting, its existence,
Quite like his doubts concerning deity
(He'd hardly give you sixpence
For any contradictory point of view);
The preconditions of experience
Need hardly give the thinker pause
In such a world where everything
(Despite the primitive desires of man),
With application and with effort can
Be shown as resting squarely on empiric laws.
I leaned upon a window sill
Set in a sky of here and now
And saw, for just the flutter of an eye,
A thing perhaps I was not meant
To see: a thousand windows
Opened down the blue,
And every space
And every time
And every sense
They gave upon
Was mine,
Yet wholly different
From anything
I knew.

After years of monumental production and financial resources dwindling, the artist takes a concluding swipe at those who find no transcendent meaning in the universe and presume their paradigms to be the arbiters of ultimate reality. *Windows for B.R.* draws from the similar window openings in both *Recapitulation* and the Bacon triptych in order to show what can reveal itself beyond the capacities of purely scientific criteria once all preconceptions dwindle to nothing and connection occurs.

***

Taylor never speaks of *Remembering the East Ranges*, his last painting, as an appropriate or conscious bookend to his early *Sparagmos* canvas with its depiction of psychic flight before cosmic collapse. It is equivalent in size and in Oriental landscape style: tiny figures on horseback returning to their ancestral lands along a vertiginous mountain trail, prepared to recover the world they had known. Their destination is not the torn and shattered world of his early Sparagmos, its human element in maddened flight, but something remembered that continues to sustain as it draws them deep into the past. (One thinks of Wordsworth's *Intimations of Immortality from Recollections of Early Childhood*, and in this connection, what a Francis Bacon might have lost at the hands of his abusive parent. Violations easily despoil such intimations and shatter the lens they provide upon the nature of existence, in other words the 'sins of the fathers' truly visiting the children.) Here the riders, barely discerned in the vast landscape, are intent on restoring the land of their memory. They will look upon it with the vision they have gained and that accompanies them. The painting is an "occasional" piece — a gift for a friend and a conclusion to Taylor's visual narrative.

Remembering the East Ranges, c. 2000
On the back of the canvas:
(Li Po's poem translated by Arthur Cooper, Chinese characters bottom left)

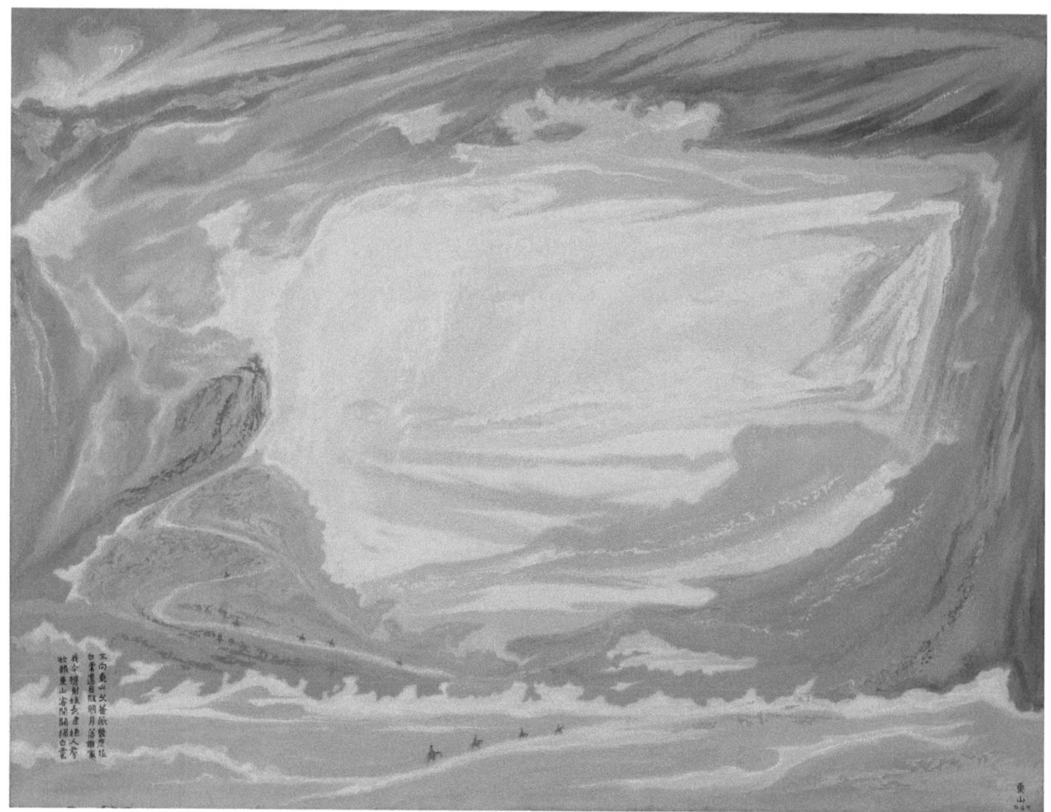

Long since I turned
to my East Ranges:
How many times
have their roses bloomed?
Have their white clouds risen and vanished
And their bright moon set among strangers?
But I shall now
take Duke Hsieh's dancers:
With a sad song
we shall leave the crowds
And call on him
in the East Ranges,
Undo the gate,
sweep back the white clouds![95]

Throughout his life, Taylor aspires to the Renaissance ideal. In its pursuit, as a young man, he writes poetry and plays, and he is a fencing duellist. He teaches himself to play classical pieces on the piano. His doctoral work satisfies three departments: Philosophy, Art and English. He teaches literature in order to finance his life as a painter. His first years lecturing at the University of Western Ontario, he produces and directs three plays to acclaim:[96] (a "colossal") Caesar and Cleopatra, Murder in the Cathedral and The Caine Mutiny Court Martial. He designs and builds his Toronto studio. Other than commissions for portraits and a Tom Thomson copy[97] that he tries to buy back, he refuses to sell any of his paintings.

Reproduction of Tom Thomson's Spring Ice, >
1992

In his final years, when large paintings are beyond his physical and financial capacity, he writes novels and books of short stories.[98] When asked what his occupation is, he replies, "I'm a painter."

***

---

[95] Arthur Cooper, *Li Po and Tu Fu: Poems Selected and Translated with an Introduction and Notes* (Penguin Books, 1973).
[96] Here one must accept the director's claims, substantiating reviews of the time unfortunately not available.
[97] The synchronicity of events leading to this commission is a story in itself as is the basis for Taylor's lengthy reflection upon the possible cosmic connection between himself and Tom Thomson. See Taylor, *The Winnowed Field,* 192–200.
[98] Novels: *A Burning Blue, Time and the Emperor, The Cellist,* and *Tales of the Aquitaine;* Short Story Collections: *Where Have All the Borgias Gone?, Sons and Brothers,* and *Windsown & Other Stories.*

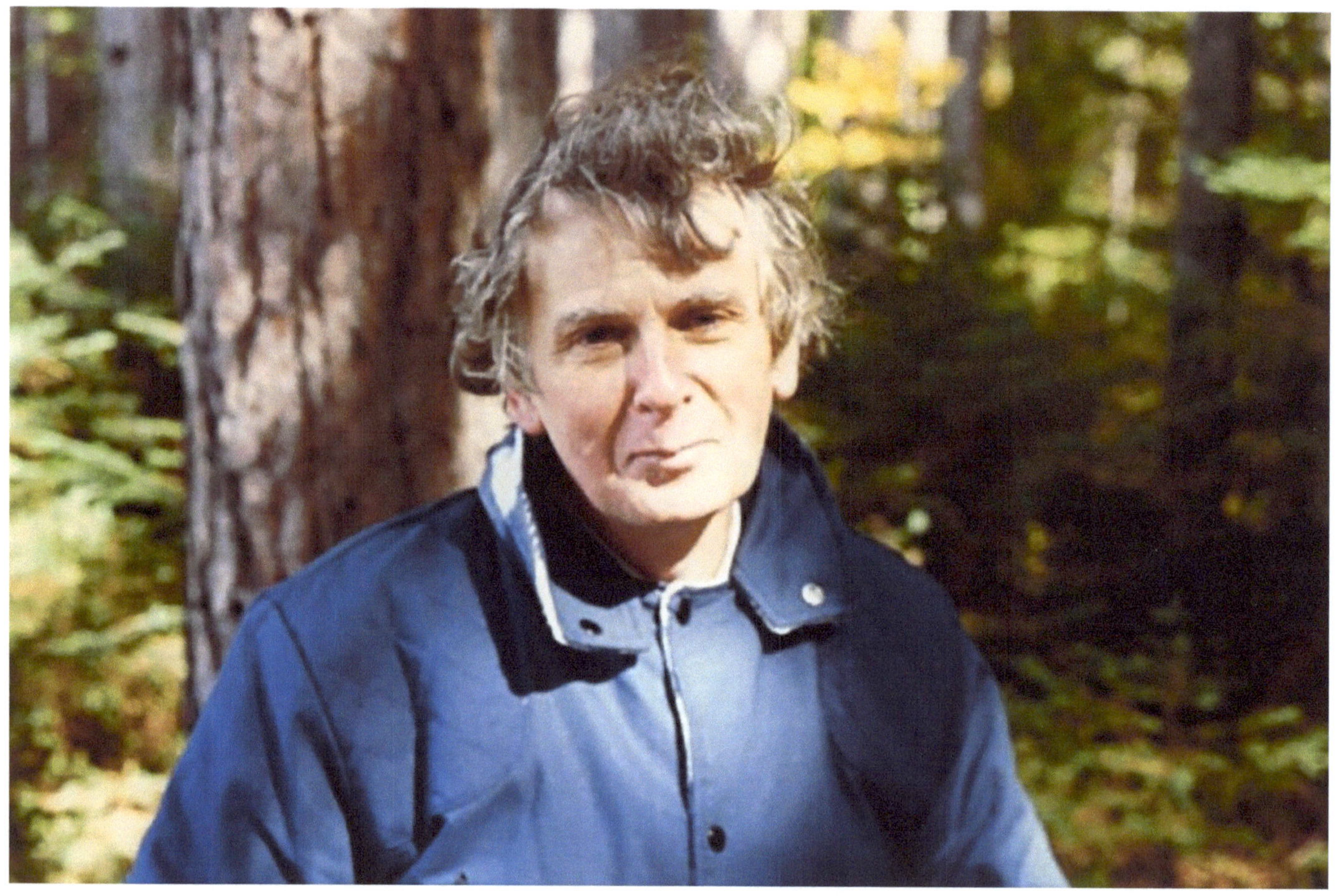

Taylor in Algonquin Park

***

Go to the Zircon Court address in what was once Willowdale (now part of North York), Ontario, and the visitor will see that the house remains but not the studio that the artist and his friend built after they removed half of the split-level roof. The studio, with its eventual clumps of dislodged parquet underfoot, no longer exists but the paintings that came out of that workplace survive. They have survived both the freezing winters when ice built up on the inside of the single-paned windows, and the greenhouse conditions of summertime; they have survived repeated rolling and re-stretching as the artist carted favourite canvases back and forth between his Montreal and Toronto studios; they have survived being dragged across the studio floor as he showed them to one visitor or another. Huge paintings, they have survived being stacked together one against the other. Finally, they survived a journey by sea to France and back in a misguided effort to find a home for them when a friend of the artist assured him that his family's chateau would be in proper repair for their safe keeping.[99] Restoration work after the artist's death has helped to ensure their survival.

---

[99] For this particular tale of woe, see Xylinides, *Sparagmos: the fall.*

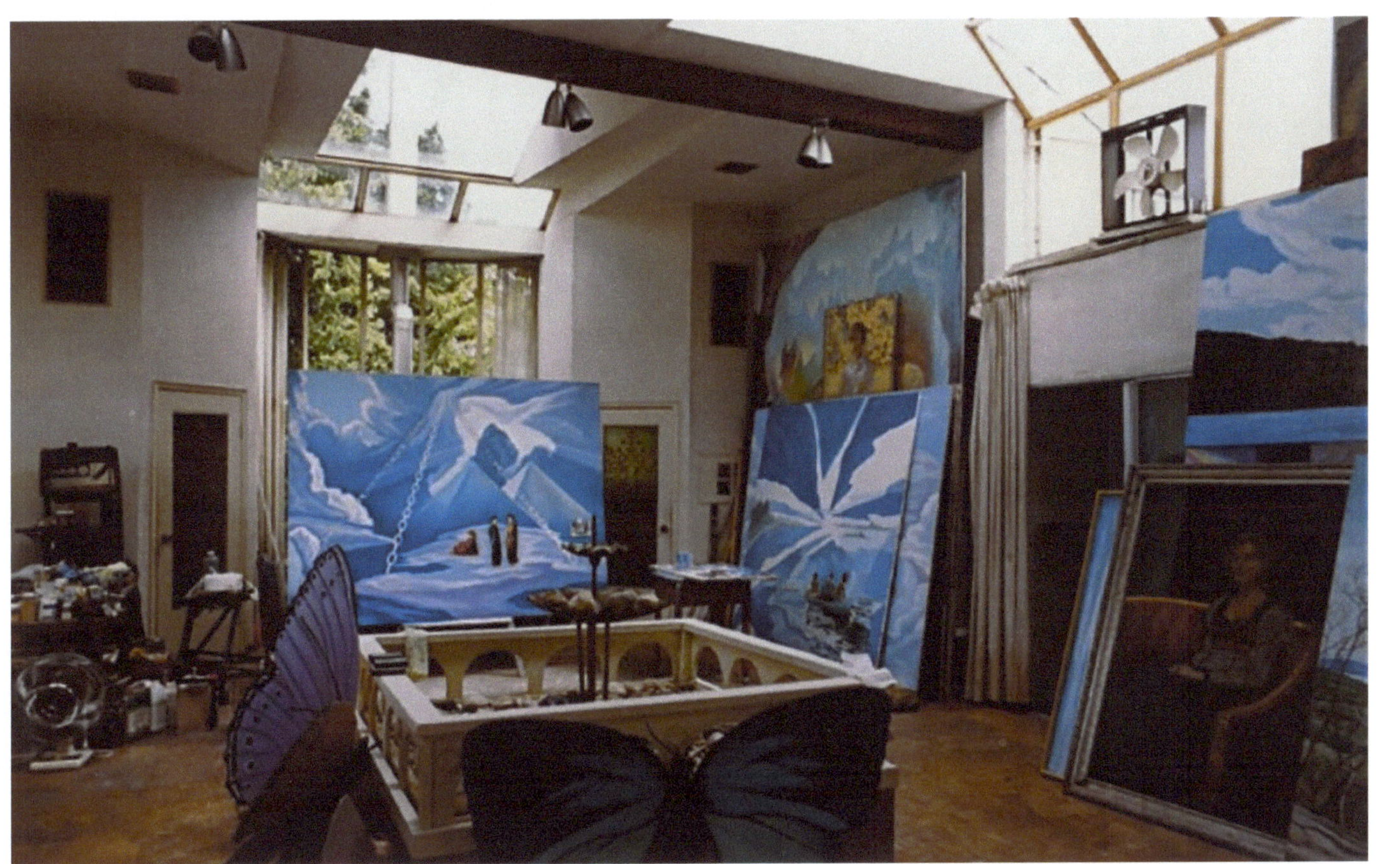

Toronto studio interior

***

Biographical Notes

1931
Born David George Taylor, September 1st, in Toronto, Ontario.

1940s
Taylor attended art classes offered at the Toronto Art Gallery (now the Art gallery of Ontario).

1955, 1958, 1969
B.A., M.A., Ph.D., University of Toronto, University College. Doctoral work under Northrop Frye and Marshall McLuhan. He satisfied two departments – Philosophy and English – for his thesis on the British art critic Roger Fry.

1958
He obtained his first teaching position and studio at Huron College, University Of Western Ontario. "There, at last, I could really paint – could attempt something large. Up to this point all of my paintings (at least those I care to own to) had been of only moderate size." (Taylor, *The Winnowed Field*).

1960

He produced his first two major works: *Peniel* and *The Sounding of the Seventh Angel*. He also designed, produced and directed student productions of *Caesar and Cleopatra, Murder in the Cathedral,* and *The Caine Mutiny Court Martial.*

1962

David wrote *The April Oyster* a play which Northrop Frye reviewed favourably.[100]

1965

Taylor moved to Montreal in order to take on a teaching position at McGill University. His second studio situated on Redpath Crescent on the side of Mount Royal proved to be ideal for painting with its tall winged ceiling and banked windows offering a southern view of the St. Lawrence River and beyond. Here he completed his doctoral work and painted most of the canvases in the visionary symbolic period.

1967

With his friend Paul Butler, he undertook a number of hiking trips into the White Mountains of New Hampshire where he found inspiration for the *Ezekiel* and *Likeness of the Ox paintings.*

1972

His first and only exhibition took place at the Unitarian Church in Toronto. The paintings on view included Peniel, *The Sounding of the Seventh Angel,* The New Jerusalem – Building of the City, and Silence. A few days after the show opened it was closed, as parishioners complained the works were "religious" and there were threats that the police would be called. (Taylor, *The Winnowed Field*). Northrop Frye, who attended, was to comment, "I didn't think you could commit sacrilege in the Unitarian Church."

Taylor's contract at McGill ended that same year, and he obtained a teaching position at Concordia University with eventual tenure.

1976–1979

Over three summers, he built his Toronto studio, with more than seventy windows, multiple skylights.

1977

He published "The Aesthetic Theories of Roger Fry Reconsidered, Journal of Aesthetics and Art Criticism", xxxvi/i Fall 1977.

---

[100] "This is an extremely well constructed comedy, refreshingly free of ironic nudging ... keeps closely to the Classical spirit appropriate to its setting ... just enough slapstick to give visual interest ... a most unusual type of thing ... I am very glad to have had an opportunity to see it." Northrop Frye, undated letter (Victoria College, Toronto, Office of the Principal, *Taylor Archives*).

1986

Taylor published "Aesthetic Personality," *International Journal of Aesthetics and Philosophy of Culture – Lier En Boog*, Volume 5, Issue 2.

1991

After availing himself of all the sabbaticals due to him (1986, 1989 and 1990 – an extra year without pay), in order to continue painting full time, Taylor accepted diminished income and took early retirement from Concordia. With his friend Paul Butler, he continued to undertake trips – now by canoe – into the wilderness: Algonquin, Quetico and Lady Evelyn Smooth Water River. These trips provided the inspiration for all of the major paintings in the visionary landscape period as well as *Paddler Floating In Time* from the earlier visionary figurative.

1991–2000

During this stage of his career, Taylor supplemented his financial resources with a number of commissioned portraits.

2001

David wrote his family memoir – *The Winnowed Field* – in which he describes his feeling of spiritual affinity with the Canadian painter Tom Thomson.

2003–2008

David published a book of short stories titled *Moriah*, and completed two more books of short stories: *The Swans* and *Something Like Ulysses* and four novels: *The Burning Blue, I Genghis, The Cellist,* and *Tales Of The Aquitane*.

2009

When his health failed him, David was forced to sell his Willowdale home and studio and return to Montreal.

2012

David Taylor died, April 2nd, in Hôtel Dieu Hospital, Montreal Quebec, a short distance from his second studio on the side of Mount Royal.

***

The Taylor paintings cited herein are selected from the complete collection. In his final years, the artist designated the canvases that comprise his core work.

List of Core Paintings

(Visionary symbolic)

PENIEL
SOUNDING OF THE SEVENTH ANGEL
BUILDING OF THE CITY, THE NEW JERUSALEM
ANGEL OF REVELATIONS X
PASSAGE OVER EDEN
SEA LILIES
VISITATION
THERE IS NO CONSTANCY IN TIME

(Visionary figurative)

PADDLER FLOATING IN TIME
PHANTASMAGORIA
THE ASSUMPTION THAT THERE IS A HORSE
IN YOUTH WE WERE VERY MUCH ADMIRED
INTERVAL BETWEEN ICE AGES
BRIDGE, DAIQUIRIS, HUMANISM, ETC.
NORTHERN PRIMAVERA
WIND-SOWN
RECAPITULATION
WEDNESDAY
THE UNIVERSE OF FRANCIS BACON
THE UNIVERSE OF FRANCIS BACON II
APOTHEOSIS OF FRANCIS BACON

(Visionary Landscape)

ANIMOOSH
CLAMSHELL LAKE
EQUINOX
SKYLIGHT STUDY
LADY EVELYN SMOOTH WATER RIVER
SILENCES JOINING, CROW RIVER STUDY I
THE DAWN STEALER, CROW RIVER STUDY II

(Additional core paintings)

WE ARE ALIVE, WE ARE GROWING
MAY
PORTRAIT OF MAX DE LA CAMP, MARQUIS DE RUSÉE D'EFFIAT
PORTRAIT OF PAUL BUTLER
AFTERNOON ON NANTUCKET

David Taylor Art Collection
(located at 110/112 Lewis Avenue, Westmount, Quebec, H3Z 2K6)
by appointment — 514 937 0910

***

Bibliography

Archimbauld, Michel, *Francis Bacon In Conversation*, Phaidon, 1993.

Farson, Daniel, *The Gilded Gutter Life of Francis Bacon*, Pantheon Books, New York, 1993.

Frye, Northrop, *Fearful Symmetry: a Study of William Blake*, ed. Nicholas Halmi, University of Toronto Press, Toronto, 2004.

Koren, Leonard, *Wabi-Sabi for Artists, Designers, Poets & Philosophers*, Stone Bridge Press, Berkeley, California, 1994.

Nicholl, Charles, *Leonardo da Vinci: Flights of the Mind*, Viking Penguin, New York, 2004.

Peppiatt, Michael, *Francis Bacon: Anatomy of an Enigma*, Skyhorse Publishing, New York, 2009.

Russell, John, *Francis Bacon*, Thames and Hudson, 1993.

Taylor, David George, "Aesthetic Personality," *International Journal of Aesthetics and Philosophy of Culture, Lier en Boog*, volume 5/issue 2.

——————————————, Catalogue, *The Sounding of the Seventh Angel*, The Collected Paintings 1956–2000.

——————————————, *Roger Fry, Critic in a Landscape, doctoral thesis*, University of Toronto.

——————————————, "The Aesthetic Theories of Roger Fry Reconsidered," *The Journal of Aesthetics and Art Criticism*, XXXVI/1, Fall 1977.

——————————————, Website: www.davidgeorgetaylor.com.

——————————————, *The Winnowed Field — a brief family history —*, handwritten, bound, David Taylor Archives.

Xylinides, Paul, *Sparagmos: the fall — a memoir —*, 2015.

Author

Paul Butler, the "student" of the text, regarded David Taylor as a mentor in all matters aesthetic and literary. He obtained his MA in English Literature from McGill University and writes novels and children's stories under his mother's maiden name Xylinides (Paul). His observations and critique of Taylor's work come from an intellectual engagement with the artist that spanned their fifty-year-long friendship as narrated in *Sparagmos: the fall* — a memoir.

Acknowledgements:

The editorial work of Dorota Kozinska (managing editor, *Vie des Arts Magazine*) and Dr. Joanne Harris Burgess has been invaluable. Lucie Ranger (translator) generously and skilfully proofed the final text and offered sensitive comments.

—